Y0-CUW-576

WITH MIND AND HEART RENEWED...

*Essays in Honor of
Rev. John F. Harvey, O.S.F.S.*

on the occasion of his 80th birthday and
the 55th anniversary of his ordination to the priesthood

Edited by
Thomas F. Dailey, O.S.F.S.

University Press of America,® Inc.
Lanham · New York · Oxford

Copyright © 2001 by
University Press of America,® Inc.
4720 Boston Way
Lanham, Maryland 20706

12 Hid's Copse Rd.
Cumnor Hill, Oxford OX2 9JJ

All rights reserved
Printed in the United States of America
British Library Cataloging in Publication Information Available

Library of Congress Cataloging-in-Publication Data

With heart and mind renewed : essays in honor of
Rev. John F. Harvey, O.S.F.S. on the occasion of his
80th birthday and the 55th anniversary of his ordination to
the priesthood / edited by Thomas F. Dailey.
p. cm
Includes bibliographical references.
1. Christian ethics—Catholic authors. 2. Pastoral theology—
Catholic Church. I. Harvey, John F. (John Francis), 1918-
II. Dailey, Thomas F.
BJ1249 .W54   2001   241'.042—dc21   2001023354 CIP

ISBN 0-7618-2000-0 (cloth: alk. paper)
ISBN 0-7618-2001-9 (pbk. : alk. paper)

∞™ The paper used in this publication meets the minimum
requirements of American National Standard for Information
Sciences—Permanence of Paper for Printed Library Materials,
ANSI Z39.48—1984

Contents

Contributors v

Introduction — The Making of a Moral Theologian
(Rev. THOMAS F. DAILEY, O.S.F.S.) 1

Part I: A Context for Moral Theology

Chapter 1 Professional Responsibility
          (Dr. JUDE DOUGHERTY) 9

Chapter 2 John Paul II and the Family: The Synod of 1980
          (Rev. Msgr. MICHAEL WRENN) 23

Chapter 3 Reflections on Salesian Anthropology
          (Rev. JOHN CROSSIN, O.S.F.S.) 39

Chapter 4 The Christian Moral Life and Evangelization:
          Contemporary Culture, Conscience, and the
          Magisterium
          (Dr. WILLIAM MAY) 59

Part II: Topics in Moral and Pastoral Theology

Chapter 5 Reviving the Sixth Commandment with
          Fr. John Harvey
          (Rev. Msgr. GEORGE A. KELLY) 81

Chapter 6	Waiting for Grace: The Pastoral Care of Those Who Are Not Yet Disposed to Follow the Commandments (Rev. BENEDICT GROESCHEL, C.F.R.) 105
Chapter 7	Biomedical Research with 'Decisionally Incapacitated' Human Subjects: Legalization of a Defunct Normative Bioethics Theory (Dr. DIANE IRVING) 119
Chapter 8	Therapy: Friend or Foe to Spiritual Values and the Sacraments (Rev. W. JEROME BRACKEN, C.P.) 143

Postscript — Thoughts from a Former Student
(Dr. ROSALIND SMITH EDMAN) 161

Bibliography — The Legacy of a Moral Theologian 165

Contributors

Rev. W. Jerome Bracken, C.P. is Associate Professor at Immaculate Conception Seminary and School of Theology.

Rev. John Crossin, O.S.F.S., formerly the President of the De Sales School of Theology (Washington, DC), is currently the Executive Director of the Washington Theological Consortium. He is the author of several books on virtue ethics.

Rev. Thomas Dailey, O.S.F.S. is Associate Professor in, and Chairman of, the Dept. of Philosophy & Theology at DeSales University (Center Valley, PA), where he also directs the Salesian Center for Faith & Culture. He also serves as the Executive Secretary of the Fellowship of Catholic Scholars.

Dr. Jude Dougherty is Professor Emeritus of Philosophy at Catholic University of America (Washington, DC), where he served as Dean of the School of Philosophy for thirty-one years. He continues to work as editor of the *Review of Metaphysics*. In 1999, he received CUA's President's Medal and was also awarded the title Knight of the Order of St. Gregory, by action of Pope John Paul II.

Dr. Rosalind Smith Edman, a former student of Fr. Harvey's at Dunbarton College (class of 1964), holds a Ph.D. from the Catholic University of America and is currently the Director of Advising at DeSales University.

Rev. Benedict Groeschel, C.F.R. is a spiritual director in the Archdiocese of New York.

Dr. DIANE IRVING is a Lecturer in the School of Philosophy at the Catholic University of America.

Rev. Msgr. GEORGE KELLY is the President Emeritus of the Fellowship of Catholic Scholars. Long-time sociologist of the American Church, he has written numerous books on the changing relationship between Catholicism and culture. For this work he was the 1999 recipient of the Pope Pius XI award from the Society of Catholic Social Scientists.

Dr. WILLIAM MAY is the Michael J. McGivney Professor of Moral Theology at the John Paul II Institute for Studies on Marriage and Family (Washington, DC). He is the author of several books on marriage, moral theology, and sexual ethics.

Rev. Msgr. MICHAEL WRENN, K.C.H.S., a Chevalier of the French Republic in the Order of Academic Palms, is currently Pastor of the Church of St. John the Evangelist (New York) and Special Consultant for Religious Education to John Cardinal O'Connor.

Introduction

The Making of a Moral Theologian

Rev. THOMAS F. DAILEY, O.S.F.S.

It all began when he was about ten years old, as he stole through a hole in the fence of old Shibe Park to watch the Philadelphia Athletics play baseball. Now, some seventy-five years later, his fanatical appreciation for and recollection of the sport has not at all changed ... only his morality!

No doubt, he could offer an erudite apologia to justify his youthful misadventure. Without hesitation he would unabashedly embrace the role of the moralist and gleefully profess what he learned from a former teacher (Francis Connell, C.SS.R.): *raro affirmare, numquam negare, semper distinguere* (rarely affirm, never negate, and always distinguish)!

Not long after his sandlot days, young John Harvey attended Northeast Catholic High School. After being graduated with the highest grade average, he then entered the novitiate of the religious congregation of priests who taught him in high school. Later, following his own ordination to the priesthood in 1944 and the completion of graduate studies, he would, in turn, become the teacher of numerous future priests in that same congregation ... and beyond.

His formal theological education took place at the Catholic University of America. There, too, his athletic interests never waned. Following a degree in psychology in 1946, he pondered the possibility of writing a dissertation on the morality of professional boxing. Some recall this as a clever ploy to deem his watching the Friday night fights as "research"! Everyone now recognizes there the beginning of that *distinguere* that would come to characterize his life-long approach to, and application of, moral theology. He would eventually complete his degree in 1951 with an analysis of Augustine's *Confessions*.

Fr. Harvey's career in moral education developed for the most part at the De Sales School of Theology (in Washington, DC), the seminary of the Oblates of St. Francis de Sales, where he taught for forty years and later served as its President. During his tenure there, he is credited with completing the school's formal accreditation by the Association of Theological Schools and with the creation of the Cluster of Independent Theological Schools. Ever the teacher, he still found time to pursue his exploits in the classroom at Dunbarton College of the Holy Cross, where he instructed young ladies for some twenty-five years.

In these various educational posts, the composite of a beloved moralist begins to emerge. On the one hand, there stood before students an orthodox theologian, one who taught with clarity and refused to yield to error. (Rumor has it he even flew to Ireland to correct the repeated misrepresentation of his teaching on a radio program there!) On the other hand, there sat with believers a caring pastor, one who embodied true Salesian humility and gentleness as he provided comfort and counsel to persons struggling to live a moral life.

That blend of prelate and mentor, of teacher and grandfather — we might say, of athlete in the game of life and loyal fan through both wins and losses — would lead him to his present labors in the field of moral and pastoral theology. In 1980 he founded the association now called "Courage"— a spiritual support group to help men and women live chaste lives, in accordance with the Church's teaching on homosexuality. The group has grown to number some eighty-four chapters, with organizations in twenty-nine dioceses in the United States, five dioceses in Canada, and other locations in the United Kingdom, the Republic of Ireland, Australia, New Zealand, and the Philippines.

Even today, while he lives at DeSales University in northeast Pennsylvania, Fr. Harvey commutes to New York City each week to direct the world-wide efforts of "Courage" and to minister to its members. From there, he returns to his beloved Philadelphia on Sundays to assist with the sacraments in a suburban parish. This routine — of teaching, guiding, and celebrating — is interrupted now and again by radio and television appearances, as well as by more global pursuits, including stints as a visiting professor in Australia and New Zealand. But each time Fr. Harvey somehow manages to find his way back home ... usually just in time to catch the end of a Phillies game on the radio!

There is no Hall of Fame specifically designated for faithful moral theologians. If there were, you would probably find there Fr. Harvey's familiar likeness — with the jovial features of a smiling Irishman, whose head of a few white hairs reflects not only the sun but the crown of an intellect still sharp and most well-read. There, too, you would hear a slew of anecdotal stories, too many to be recounted in these few pages, about one who could readily pinch-hit for the absent-minded professor!

But his stats would easily justify his inclusion there ... just ask any of the countless persons of every age and state-in-life who have benefitted from the wit and wisdom of his moral and spiritual guidance. His pastoral work has been noted by the conferral of two honorary doctoral degrees, his distinguished writings on morality garnered the *Linacre Quarterly* award, and his outstanding service in the Church led to his being granted the prestigious Cardinal Wright Award from the Fellowship of Catholic Scholars.

In the pages that follow, a handful of fellow scholars pay tribute to Fr. John Harvey on the occasion of his 80th birthday and the 55th anniversary of his ordination to the priesthood. They do so in a way befitting the educator that Fr. Harvey is — with works of sound scholarship and pastoral application that continue to bring moral theology to life in the minds and hearts and souls of the faithful.

The first half of the book begins with articles that provide a commentary on the theological context within which moral theology is done. In the lead-off chapter, **Jude Dougherty**, long-time dean of Philosophy at the Catholic University of America, repeats his previously published thoughts on the authority and responsibility incumbent upon any professional. In every respect, Fr. John Harvey is a professional theologian, one whose work fulfills what Prof. Dougherty calls "the professional's first obligation," namely, the duty "to excellence in his calling."

This calling is exercised, necessarily, within the Church and in light of its mission. **Msgr. Michael Wrenn**, in a previously published work, highlights the interaction of "doctrinal" and "pastoral" approaches that surrounded the Synod on Marriage and the Family and the subsequent publication of the Apostolic Exhortation on this topic. As a loyal son of the Church, Fr. Harvey has long sought to integrate the orthodox teaching of the Church and the real-life experiences of those for whom he has such great pastoral solicitude.

This integration of theological approaches also issues from the particular spirituality to which Fr. Harvey's religious life has been dedicated. **Fr. John Crossin**, a confrere of Fr. Harvey and his successor as president of the De Sales School of Theology, shares his reflections on the human person, particularly as this is understood in the spiritual tradition of St. Francis de Sales and St. Jane de Chantal. To quote from his introduction: "For over fifty years, Father Harvey has engaged in effective pastoral relationships with others. He has manifested the virtue of love in serving others. A reflection on human identity and relationality seems very appropriate in the context of honoring him." No doubt, all would agree!

Finally, Fr. Harvey's longtime colleague in Washington, **Dr. William May**, offers a contemporary viewpoint on the moral life, as this concerns the mutual relation between one's own conscience and the teaching authority of the Church. Evangelizing others to "know who we are and what we are to do if we are to be fully the beings we are meant to be" has been Fr. Harvey's life-long task, both in and out of academia.

The second half of the book treats a variety of topics in moral and pastoral theology that touch upon the life's work of Fr. Harvey. To begin, **Msgr. George A. Kelly** offers a far-reaching overview of the development of homosexuality as a social question and gives a critical commentary on the moral status of overt homosexual conduct. This chapter situates Fr. Harvey's ongoing work in its historical context and upholds his pastoral efforts as exemplary in terms of how to "build a road to virtue graced with authentic Catholic structures."

Pastoral care is also the subject taken up by **Fr. Benedict Groeschel**, a popular and well-known spiritual director in the Archdiocese of New York. His contribution addresses a question that goes to the heart of Fr. Harvey's ministry: What can be done for people in need of pastoral care without inadvertently enabling them to continue in their state of sin? In a "tolerant" society such as ours, the question demands consideration, and the method which Fr. Harvey has employed in his ministries deserves attention as a model for all those engaged in pastoral work.

A growing area of concern in pastoral theology has to do with research on human beings, the subject of an exposé by **Dr. Diane Irving**. In a piece originally prepared for publication in a law journal, she offers an analysis of proposed legislation concerning handicapped persons and therein reveals the moralist's constant attention to terminology and to the implications that follow from the confused or distorted use of terms in legal or research documents. This study shows that the acuity of the "teacher" in Fr. Harvey has now been passed on to a new generation of thinkers!

The last chapter takes up an important theme in the teacher's published work — namely, the relation between spiritual and psychological values. Here **Fr. Jerome Bracken, CP** seeks to facilitate the potentially beneficial communication between therapist and clergyman. It is a conversation that has emerged, is encouraged, and continues to be enfleshed in the life and work of Fr. John Harvey.

The collection ends with a postscript of recollections from one of Fr. Harvey's former students at Dunbarton College (**Dr. Rosalind Smith Edman**). It is the last word, in terms of this book of essays, but certainly not the final word on our honoree. For the life and work of Fr. John Harvey continue to bear fruit in the Church today ... and, hopefully, for many tomorrows.

While we might wish him the length of days needed to see the Phillies win another World Series, Fr. Harvey would rather welcome this blessing bestowed upon the faithful priest he has always been ...

Ad multos annos!

Part I:

A Context for Moral Theology

Chapter 1

Professional Responsibility [1]

Dr. JUDE P. DOUGHERTY

Few would deny that Immanuel Kant is one of a small band of great knowers. Among his lasting contributions to the study of philosophy is his *Metaphysics of Morals*. His discussion of virtue, of one's duties toward one's self and towards others is time transcending. Kant is convinced that "a doctrine of virtue is ... something that can be taught."[2] But virtue cannot be taught merely by concepts of duty or exhortations. Instead, it must be exercised and cultivated by effort. One cannot straight away do all that one wants to do. But the decision to embark on a virtuous path "must be made all at once and completely."[3] To form a habit is to establish a lasting inclination apart from any maxim. The emphasis is on inclination, but Kant was not opposed to the enunciation of maxims, provided they issued from systematic and empirical inquiry. Kant's emphasis on dialogue in the methodical treatment of virtue has found favor with many contemporary moralists as they prepare textbooks and anthologies. This is no more evident than in discussions of morality as it pertains to the professions, particularly the medical, legal and

---

[1] This article appeared in the October 1996 issue (vol. 11, no. 10) of *The World & I*, a publication of The Washington Times Corporation, copyright © 1996 and reprinted with permission.

[2] *The Metaphysics of Morals*, trans. Mary Gregor (Oxford: Oxford University Press, 1995), p. 266.

[3] *The Metaphysics of Morals*, p. 266.

academic professions. The following discussion focuses upon the concept of professional responsibility, in a generic way. It suggests, in a Kantian manner, virtues appropriate to the professions singled out for treatment.

Professional responsibility is a composite of virtues. It is a moral requirement coextensive with the authority and power conferred by office. I can not think of a moral virtue that a responsible professional ought not to have, but there are certain virtues associated with the professions which in their absence may cause some consternation. I will focus on these in a moment. But first let me say what is commonly meant by "profession" and then by "responsibility."

Defining the Terms

Though we are inclined to use the word "profession" loosely, not every occupation is rightly called professional. The etymology of the term and its historical usage may be of some help in securing a manageable definition. The term traditionally was assigned to those callings in which one "professes" to have acquired some special knowledge, useful either by way of instruction or guidance, and secondarily to those arts or services that depend upon such knowledge. In antiquity this was thought to rule out purely commercial, mechanical, agricultural or other similar occupations. Three time honored professions, theology, law and medicine were accorded the designation "learned." Although antiquity recognized only a short list of professions, contemporary claims to professional status are numerous indeed, and one would be foolhardy if he attempted to arbitrate what is and what is not rightly called a profession. Obviously, the list of professions recognized in antiquity may be expanded by a kind of analogy to many occupations. Given our ability to define them, these occupations have status, commensurate with their intellectual component, their importance to the community and their history. We normally do not look upon an electrician or a plumber as a professional, although we respect tradesmen and their craft. A profession obviously entails a theoretical dimension.

The word "responsibility" itself may give us a clue. Although the etymology of the word may be obscure, there is reason to believe that it comes from the Latin *respondeo*, similar to the French *répondre*, as in RSVP. In its Latin origin, it implies an amenability, a disposition to answer to a call. To be responsible is to be answerable. "Responsible" as an adjective denotes what Aristotle called *phronimos*, reasonableness and reliability. As a moral quality it is not confined to any particular situation but designates a disposition and perhaps a role.

Professional responsibility entails not only a disposition but a cluster of virtues. Some of these relate to the profession, some to the person *qua* person. Professional integrity depends in part on the maintenance of appropriate skills at the highest level. To be *au courant* one must be abreast of the current literature in the field, and perhaps a regular at conventions and other updating sessions. While the maintenance of professional skills is of the highest priority, technique alone is rarely sufficient for success in the long run. There is an obligation to truth about one's profession. One needs to know something about its history, where it fits into the larger schema of knowledge and activity. The value of an acquaintance with the history of the profession may vary from one discipline to another, but some knowledge of lineage is required for identity. So, too, is a regard for the future. We have an obligation to those who would succeed us. The very notion "profession" implies continuity through time, past, present and future. Indeed, one can write a history of medicine, of law, or of the priesthood. We can and do discuss or speculate about the likely future of engineering or nursing as a profession. The perception of long-range needs will determine our action now.

It is hard to imagine any endeavor which may be called professional which does not involve this learned or cognitive dimension. In the traditionally recognized professions, theology, law, and medicine, a premium was placed on learning. The obvious relation between learning and achievement is seen historically wherever we find the knowledgeable sought for judgeships, administrative positions or bishoprics. From Ambrose to Kilwarby to Scalia we find examples. So, too, in contemporary professions unknown to antiquity.

Just as there are many varieties and many degrees of authority and many mechanisms for conferral, one achieves responsibility in as many ways. The most obvious is by virtue of elected or appointed office, certainly, but in other ways, too. By virtue of authorship, the parent is responsible for the child, even *in utero*, and those who are parents may wonder whether that responsibility ever ceases. Kinship evokes a kind of responsibility quite apart from legal and even moral responsibility. Within the modern corporation, from the building engineer to the chief executive officer, there are levels of responsibility, and even within those levels there may be degrees of responsibility. Similarly, within a profession there are degrees of responsibility.

To develop a theme just mentioned, it is evident that the professional's first obligation is to excellence in his calling. He has an obligation not only to the mastery of relevant technique, and in some professions ever changing techniques, but to the theoretical dimension of his work. The recognition of those truths, which bear upon the fundamental features of his work and of the relation of that work to life as a whole is a part of the speculative and practical wisdom required of the professional. Praxis is grounded in theoria. One needs normative principles in order to judge and to evaluate. These are most likely to come from sources outside the empirical present. Experience garnered from the past is indispensable if one is to recognize that there are certain laws governing nature and human behavior that remain invariant through generations, indeed through millennia. In almost every profession, to be steeped in its history is to possess a vantage point. One cannot claim status as an economist without having read Adam Smith.

In some disciplines and consequently in some professions a knowledge of the history of the discipline is more important than in others. Human nature like nature itself has not changed from antiquity. Whereas the natural sciences have advanced on the back of developments in technology, there have been no technological innovations which have brought us closer to an examination of human nature. Thus it behooves us to read and reread works such as Aristotle's *Nicomachean Ethics* and his *Politics*, Cicero on *The Commonwealth*, and Augustine on *The City of God*. If standards are not to be trivial, they will in some sense have to transcend the present and rest upon the best judgments available to the race. If practices are to be judged, if the manners and customs of a profession or even of a people are to be evaluated, there will have to be a means of achieving a perspective that will enable such assessments to take place. Livy said as much for the Rome of his day which by the first century B.C. was already conscious of its past. "What chiefly makes the study of history wholesome and profitable is this, that in history you have a record of the infinite variety of human experience plainly set out for all to see, and in that record you can find for yourself and your country both examples and warning."[4]

Concerning the nature of law and the responsibilities of the magistrate, Cicero remains a guide. For Cicero the highest expression of profes-

---

[4] Preface to his *History* (Cambridge, MA: Loeb Classical Library, 1924), vol. 1, p. 7.

sional life is the care of the public, a vocation he accepted for himself. In *De Officiis*, distinguishing between community service and individual advancement, he makes a high-minded distinction between the "*bonnum honestum*" and the "*bonnum utile*," identifying the former with the common good and the latter with individual interest.[5] What is just serves the *res publica*. Just as self interest should not be placed above the common good, the calculations of special interest groups should not be placed above the good of the commonwealth. Cicero's emphasis on communal responsibility is so strong that he has often been used to justify overstepping the bounds of law in the pursuit of the common good.

Following Cicero's line of argument, both wisdom and prudence are requisite for he who would assume responsibility in the commonwealth. He who would work for the common good must be able to distinguish between what is truly good and that which has only apparent usefulness. A person in authority must strive always for the just, but it must be acknowledged that, measured against the standard of absolute good, many of his actions will fall short. The just or equitable is principled and bears in mind long range effects. The pursuit of utility, disengaged from any notion of *honestum*, threatens the viability of society. Self-preservation depends on the commonwealth; the defense of society is thus the highest priority.

The contemporary relevance of this Ciceronian treatise does not escape us. The rule of law takes precedence, but the principles upon which the law rests are themselves derivative. They presuppose a philosophy and a tradition. Recognition of a divine order is explicit in Cicero. He emphasizes the requirement of learning and respect for the inherited; he takes for granted the commonness of the human condition and on it bases his respect for the lessons of history. Every commonwealth, he proclaims, if it aims to maintain itself in being, requires its tradition. The same can be said here and now of our own commonwealth and of its organizations and professions.

Evidence of the exercise of professional responsibility is to be found in every age. Take the three learned professions. The oath attributed to the ancient Greek physician Hippocrates, adopted throughout the centuries as a guide for conduct in the medical profession, is one still used during graduation ceremonies at many universities and schools of

---

[5] *On the Commonwealth*, translated with an introduction by C.H. Sabine and S.B. Smith (Indianapolis: Bobbs-Merrill, 1950).

medicine. The first in the book of *Aphorisims* attributed to Hippocrates reads, "Life is short, and the art long; opportunity fleeting; experiment dangerous and judgment difficult."[6] One can say the same of many professions. Their art is indeed long, meaning they have a history. Often the opportunity to act, regrettably, is fleeting. In times of crisis who does not recognize that the tried and the true provides a standard? And who has not experienced that the prudential judgment is fraught with danger; there are no rules respecting the application of rules. Hippocrates can not be gainsaid.

The oaths, codes and rules of professional conduct that have been adopted by the major professions over the centuries may be taken as an expression of collective responsibility. The Hippocratic oath is only the most famous. Rabbinical codes antedate Christianity. Rules and codes governing the conduct of ecclesiastics from the early centuries of Christianity still prevail or have their contemporary counterparts. Benedict's rule is the epitome of common sense. Legal fraternities offer another example of the adoption and even the enforcement of codes of practice.

The legal profession in the United States as early as the 18th century developed a code of conduct relevant to professional activities. For many years this code was unwritten, but in the late 19th century some jurisdictions began to adopt written codes by rule of court. Shortly after the turn of this century the American Bar Association proposed a series of written canons which, updated in 1970, almost universally have been adopted throughout the United States. The current *Code of Professional Responsibility* is divided into three parts: 1) Canons, or axiomatic statements, expressing general standards of professional conduct; 2) Ethical considerations deemed relevant; and 3) Disciplinary rules, which are regarded as mandatory in character, and which have the force of law in most jurisdictions. The 1970 Code was amplified by the "Model Rules of Professional Conduct." Adopted by the American Bar Association in 1983, it may be considered to be a gloss on the earlier code. Citing just a few of the Canons will suggest their nature. Canon I asserts that a lawyer should assist in maintaining the integrity and competence of the legal profession; Canon IV, a lawyer should preserve the confidences and secrets of a client; Canon V, a lawyer should exercise independent professional judgment on behalf of a client; Canon VIII, a lawyer should

---

[6] *The New Encyclopedia Britannica*, "Medicine, History of," vol. 11, p. 827.

assist in improving the legal system; Canon IX, a lawyer should avoid even the appearance of professional impropriety. These Canons may be viewed as rules of reason which are applicable analogously to other professions.[7]

On Authority

Responsibility follows upon authority and the power commensurate with it. But authority is achieved in a multiplicity of ways. *De jure* authority is achieved by virtue of appointed or elective office, but other kinds of authority need to be recognized. Print and visual media are cases in point. The authority of the media is in part self conferred (*The New York Times* proclaims itself to be "the paper of record"), and in part conferred by a readership, or by "viewers like you," as the expression goes.

An important type of authority is that which comes with the mastery of a discipline or a technique, one that is sometimes called "epistemic" authority. And while epistemic authority is self-generated, once recognized it carries with it commensurate responsibility. The acknowledged authority cannot be loose or careless in speech or in print. The less informed depend upon the precision and carefulness of the acknowledged master. Any sloppiness allowed in the line of reports, judgment or advice is thought to be a betrayal. People do and must rely on authorities.

What we take to be true of an individual's responsibility is true of a group or of a profession as a whole. Advertisers often attempt to transfer epistemic authority from its recognized domain to the endorsement of a specific product. The man in the white coat is a familiar television personality. In the late thirties when a group of scientists for reasons of national security wanted to get President Roosevelt's attention, they drafted a letter for the signature of one of the best known mathematical physicists of the day. The physicist's authority was sufficient to gain the attention sought. Epistemic authority was recognized and the message conveyed was acted upon. As we know, the Manhattan Project changed the course of the war in the Pacific.

But, beyond the *de jure*, and that based on cognitive skills, there is another kind of authority often called "moral" or "charismatic," although the two may not be the same thing. The person who with rhetorical skill

---

[7] *Multistate Professional Responsibility* (SMH Inc., 1987), pp. 17-84.

can dramatically call attention to a moral principle can often wield a tremendous amount of power. While we may be hesitant to call this professional, it is a power frequently found in one who holds office, for example, Dr. Spock in the medical profession, Mahatma Gandhi in the political, or Mother Teresa in the social order. The authority of John Paul II, to the extent that it carries beyond the Church he leads, may be considered as a further example.

There is yet another kind of authority, recognizable, but difficult to define. It flows from an affective disposition, Kant's bottom line "good will," you may say, which leads to "caring," "solicitude," or "concern" and the assumption of responsibility, for example, for one's co-workers, fraternity, or community. Something like this is found in an extended family where members may have very little contact with each other over the course of a year, but respond in an emergency with surprising solicitude. The responsible daughter, brother, aunt, though separated by distance and the benefit of frequent visits, nevertheless assume duties that neighbors and close friends do not recognize as obligations. The recognition of duty to one's kinfolk is certainly an exercise in responsibility, although not of professional responsibility. Still the same disposition has effects in civic order and in one's profession. Cicero located the foundation of a desire for justice in our natural inclination to love our fellow man.[8] Kant recognized that a sense of duty and self-control are the personal moral dispositions which make concerted or communal action possible. Our moral sentiments dispose us to act, but not in any particular direction; they arise in the context of our natural sociability and are affected by the prevailing culture. On the downside, it takes little experience to recognize that without the guidance of a body of settled norms sentiment can wreck havoc. Under the disposition of sympathy or in the name of fairness, a society can destroy itself. Without a standard or a hierarchical ordering of ends, all claims tend to be equated. Without the recognition of time-transcending moral norms, decisions are likely to be ad hoc, resulting in an incoherent pattern of action. Responsible action, personal or communal, entails accountability, even when motivated by compassion. We may not be accountable to any person or authority, but still recognize our accountability to an independent moral order. Who or what defines that order is another topic. In the East, it may be a Confucian tradition; in the West it is likely to be carried by

---

[8] *Laws* I, 5, 16.

Christianity. Philosophy has been notoriously weak in carrying moral norms.

Of some professions we expect exemplary behavior. Physicians for the most part still take the Hippocratic oath, members of the bar undergo scrutiny for moral uprightness, and there are clearly defined codes of behavior for military personnel. Clergy, most of all, are held to very high moral standards.

A Context for Responsible Action

A responsible person acts within a context. Moral agency implies free will, intentionality, and a moral order independent of one's making. As a manifestation of his freedom, a moral person does not deny agency but accepts responsibility for his actions. His involvement for good or bad, brings praise or blame. Recognizing accountability, the moral agent thinks about what he is doing, and acts for reasons that he thinks are professionally proper rather than for reasons he would be ashamed to acknowledge. Considerations of accountability militate against the thoughtless or impulsive act. With sufficient thought, one takes care to perform those acts which must be done and not to leave anything undone that needs to be done. If anything goes amiss, the moral agent must be prepared to put things right again. A responsible person is one who can be left in charge, one who can be relied upon to perform, one who will not leave the job undone or be distracted from the business at hand. The responsible honor obligations in the absence of rewards for doing so and in the absence of sanctions for failure.

Assuming responsibility may not be the most pleasant of undertakings. Acting from responsibility can lead to the charge that one is unfriendly, unsympathetic or worse. Yet a person would be imprudent who is so unfailingly sympathetic as to give aid and comfort to even the most devious of supplicants. When placed in competition with one's natural sociability and the desire to be liked, responsibility may lose out. We are inclined to ambiguity in an effort to protect the feelings of a friend or those of the disadvantaged. Yet the responsible person will pursue the difficult good, even if this means that he is the bearer of bad news or the instrument of discipline.

The right course of behavior is not always self-evident. There is a distinction to be made between wisdom and prudence. In deliberating, the relevant principle may be clear, but the application of that principle is something else. Thus when we decide, in difficult cases at least, we take to thought. We weigh considerations pro and con and assess the balance of the competing options. Once we have reached a decision, we are prepared to explain and justify it by citing the principle we have observed and by offering reasons for coming down one way rather than another. Sometimes our decision seems more inevitable than it really was. In looking back on it, we forget the negative factors which could have led us to decide the other way. This lapse of memory is not to be confused with a lack of freedom.

The process we know only too well from personal decisions. As J.R. Lucas reminds us in his admirable book length study of responsibility, "Reasoning about practical affairs is dialectical, that is, two-sided. It is not a matter of drawing conclusions which must, on pain of inconsistency, be conceded once the premises are admitted, but a matter of argument and counter-argument."[9] The prima facie case is mentally rebutted. The perfectly reasonable argument may be effectively countered on further consideration. We recognize that claims about reality are inherently corrigible. We may always want more information, but as often as not a decision has to be taken on the information available. Sometimes it is more important to act than to be absolutely sure that one is taking the proper course of action.

This leads us to another consideration. Since reasons are inherently shareable, actions which are implementations of reason are shareable too. I can take responsibility for an action without depriving you of responsibility for it too. I can be held responsible for an action you performed without your being any less responsible. We may be collectively responsible. If I ask you, or suggest to you, or recommend that you do something, I can be held responsible, though that does not of itself exclude your being responsible too. To take a similar scenario, suppose I am not the originator of the action, but merely go along with it. My assent may be ephemeral; we may be associated in a common enterprise, be close colleagues, or be members of the same family. When policy is debated it is reasonable to assume that each of us has an obligation to speak out, and in cases where we have not done so, it may be inferred that we approve of what is done. In the professional order it may be necessary to become engaged in the drafting of resolutions which are to be promulgated in the name of the profession. It may be necessary to

---

[9] *Responsibility* (Oxford: Clarendon Press, 1993), p. 59.

challenge groups within a profession from authorizing documents immoral in themselves or inappropriate to the role of the organization. In some instances resignation from the professional organization may be the only means to register dissent.

One cannot be responsible for everything which may flow from one's action. A man is responsible for all the consequences that he can reasonably foresee as flowing from his act. The professional moral agent has an obligation to deliberate about likely outcomes. Conversely, in judging the moral action of another one must take account of its intent. But intent is not everything. Good intentions will not redeem the intrinsically immoral act. Circumstances may color responsibility, both in a positive and in a negative fashion. In fact we are often blamed for things beyond our control; and conversely we are sometimes given greater credit than we deserve. In the matter of intention we must look beyond the horizon. *Utile* may not be the same as *honestum*. In collective action it makes no difference whether the consequences flow from one's own act taken by itself, or in conjunction with the acts of others. As Lucas puts it, "Responsibility is not like pie. There is always enough to go around; and the size of each piece is independent of the number of persons involved."[10]

Professions as a whole can be responsible or irresponsible. Positive and negative illustrations abound. One may wonder if the American Medical Association behaved responsibly, when in 1994 under pressure from the Gay and Lesbian Medical Association it reversed a time honored policy by calling for a "non judgmental recognition of sexual orientation by physicians." The same may be asked of the prior action of The American Psychiatric Association which until 1973 regarded homosexuality as a treatable form of mental illness.[11]

Examples of professional irresponsibility can be multiplied. Clergymen take sexual advantage of the young, psychiatrists of the helplessness of their patients, lawyers of the ignorance of their clients, professors of the innocence of their students. Many fail not only to observe professional codes of behavior, but jeopardize themselves before criminal law as well.

---

[10] Cf. *Responsibility*, "Shared and Collective Responsibility," pp. 75-85.

[11] American Psychiatric Report, *Washington Times* (Dec. 22, 1994), p. A9.

Perhaps the most notorious flaunting of professional standards is to be found in the media. Media personnel often identify themselves as members of "the fourth estate." By any definition they certainly qualify as professionals. A survey completed by S. Robert Lichter and Stanley Rothman (1980) reported the moral and political views of more than 240 persons whom they describe as not aspirants to stature but as members of the elite media in the United States. Among the many outlooks they uncovered, they found that members of the media, on the whole, recognize the tremendous influence they have, but nevertheless think that they should have even more influence. This sought for influence is obviously of a tutorial sort. It is not based on money or political power but on the information and ideas the media transmit to social and political leaders and to the general public.[12]

One would be innocent indeed if one thought that the media is without a social or cultural agenda. Lichter and Rothman found that for the leading journalists they interviewed, liberal views on contemporary social and political issues overwhelmingly prevailed. Quoting from their 1980 study:

> The pointed views of the national media elite are not mere wishes and opinions of those aspiring to power, but the voice of a new leadership group that has arrived as a major force in American society. Cosmopolitan in their origins, liberal in their outlooks, they are aware and protective of their collective influence. The rise of this elite has hardly gone unnoticed. Some hail them as the public's tribunes against the powerful - indispensable champions of the underdog and the oppressed. Others decry them for allegiance to an adversary culture that is chiseling away at traditional values.[13]

There are few sides of life with which the media does not deal. One would think that wielders of such a power would acknowledge and accept the responsibility to be truthful in word and image, avoiding among other vices, distortion, character assassination, and propaganda designed to alter public attitudes. Yet the reverse seems to be true. In the judgment of those who professionally follow the media, we rarely find a scrupulos-

---

[12] *Public Opinion* (October/November, 1981), p. 60.

[13] *Prime Time: How T.V. Portrays American Culture*, by S.R. Lichter, L. Lichter and S. Rothman (Regnery, 1994).

ity in the pursuit of truth, a willingness to admit error, or a consciousness of consequences.

Fourteen years after their initial study, Lichter and Rothman, joined now by Lichter's wife, returned to study the media, focusing this time exclusively on television in the United States. While their 1980 study was non-judgmental, their 1994 study does not refrain from moral assessment. In their judgment, T.V. has fallen from whatever moral balance it may have formerly possessed. They base their assessment on evidence found in an excessive depiction of violence, a failure to disapprove of or question pre-marital sex or sex under any circumstances, and in television's lampooning of anyone who criticizes homosexual lives.[14]

Rescinding from the media, who has not experienced sometimes heroic efforts of individual physicians, teachers, and members of the clergy who have acted not only in the line of duty but also beyond the call of duty? But most of the time professional responsibility is exercised in a pedestrian manner. Two minor examples come to mind to illustrate what I take to be professional responsibility. "Deaccessioning" is the term used by museums of art when they decide to sell a holding to enhance their endowment, often to make a specific purchase or to meet operating expenses. The art world as a whole seems uncomfortable with the deaccessioning practice, which often entails the betrayal of the intent of a long deceased patron. In an exercise of professional responsibility, the American Association of Museums and the American Association for State and Local History have explicitly condemned the practice, although both associations recognize that there may be very legitimate reasons for deaccessioning.

A second example: the medical profession through its pharmaceutical component has instituted practices which in the delivery of medication look to long-range outcomes, side effects and the compatibility of multiple prescriptions. Computer programs signal danger. For the busy physician it may become a fail safe mechanism. The cynic many say the system was introduced to avoid litigation, but more likely it is an expression of professional and collective responsibility, with manufacturer, physician and pharmacist cooperating to ensure favorable outcomes.

---

[14] *Prime Time* (note 13, above).

The Larger Picture

Physicist Erwin Schröedinger once wrote to his colleague Hans Reichenbach, "In the end, one has to keep it clear that all specialized knowledge has significance only in relation to one's sense of the whole."[15] What is true of physics can be said of the vocation of any professional. The professional's expertise, objectives and responsibility are one thing, but the profession exists within a larger social or cultural context. Presumably the profession exists not to enhance its practitioners, although it may certainly do so, but to serve a community or society at large. Its standards fall within that society's conception of good, that is, the goals communally pursued. Plato's remark "What is honored in a community will be cultivated there," comes to mind. Any profession may be corrupted when inappropriate, perhaps idealistic, goals are held out for its members. Can a nation or regime be corrupted? The answer seems to be "yes." One can think of Germany under Hitler, the Soviet Union under Stalin, Cuba under Castro. Under those regimes it is easy to find numerous examples of the subordination by professionals to political aims. In the field of philosophy we have the famous capitulation of Heidegger to the regime. Chemists, physicists, engineers, on all sides of the conflict we know as World War II responded to the demands of the war machine. Self interest in some cases, no doubt, but one can believe that for the most part the response was patriotic.

This leads me to my final point. The professional needs to attend to the larger scheme of morality. Like anyone else, the professional can not avoid the Socratic quest for wisdom, to know oneself in relation to self, to nature, to others and to God. Professional responsibility entails not only a mastery of technique but attention to what Russell Kirk called "the permanent things." The permanent things are the locus of any endeavor. In expressing the time-transcendent they are often the guide to communal and personal fulfillment.

---

[15] October 25, 1926, University of Pittsburgh Archives. "Denn schliesslich muss man sich darüber klar sein, dass alle Spezialerkenntnis über-haupt *nur* im grossen Zusammenhang des Weltbildes Bedeutung und Interesse hat." (Quoted with permission of the University of Pittsburgh. All rights reserved.)

Chapter Two

John Paul II and the Family:
The Synod of 1980 [1]

Rev. Msgr. MICHAEL J. WRENN, K.H.S.

In 1965, Pope Paul VI established the Synod of Bishops as a permanently constituted body charged with advising the Holy Father on issues of importance to the entire Church. In addition to its four previous general sessions in 1967 (on the Revision of the Code of Canon Law), 1971 (on Social Justice and the Ministerial Priesthood), 1974 (on Evangelization) and 1977 (on Catechetics), the Synod held an extraordinary session in 1969 (on Mixed Marriages).

There were 216 voting members to the Synod on the Family of 1980, which included thirteen patriarchs, twenty-one cardinals and bishops appointed by the Holy Father, ten general superiors of religious orders, and one hundred and forty-eight elected delegates from five continents and one hundred and five countries. Each National Bishops Conference enjoys the right to elect one delegate for every twenty-five bishops up to a maximum of four delegates. In countries such as the United States with more than one hundred bishops, the Holy Father usually adds an additional delegate; in this instance, Terence Cardinal Cooke, Archbishop of New York, was designated a papal appointee.

---

[1] Previously published as the preface to *Pope John Paul II and the Family*, ed. Rev. Michael J. Wrenn (Qunicy, IL: Franciscan Press, 1982) and reprinted here with permission of the publisher.

The synod of 1980 also included forty-three auditors, of whom sixteen were married couples, three priests, four nuns and four additional lay people. There were also ten experts appointed as advisors by the Secretariat of the Synod.

Although the official language of the sessions is Latin, five modern languages may be used: English, French, German, Italian and Spanish, with provisions for simultaneous translation into all the working languages.

Even if they know how this recent postconciliar vehicle for collegial dialogue came about, many Catholics probably view the synod of the world's bishops as a meeting which lasts a mere two or three weeks in Rome every few years. Television coverage is usually restricted to the opening and closing ceremonies connected with the event, and journalists tend to capitalize upon the headline-making potential of synodal interventions which could be interpreted as running counter to traditional Church practice and teaching. Actually, this seems to have become an almost unwritten law governing most journalistic coverage of matters Roman Catholic, especially in the United States. During the 1980 Synod, it truly seemed as though the major newspapers and magazines were keeping a running score regarding issues connected with the Church's faith and practice in the realm of marriage and family life.

The fact, however, is that a Synod is conducted over a period of years beginning with a vast preparation on many different levels. In the case of the recent Synod, the Roman-based Permanent Council of the Synod, assisted by its Secretary General, sent out two preliminary documents to Episcopal conferences throughout the world. This first document, entitled "The Role of the Christian Family in Today's World," formed the basis of study and discussion with Episcopal conferences and also served as a means of consultation with the faithful of individual countries. The various responses from Episcopal conferences were examined in January, 1980, and figured prominently in the elaboration of the *Instrumentum Laboris* (working document) which was sent to the National Bishops Conferences in the Spring of that year.

It is important to note that, from an organizational point of view, there is a great deal of difference between the procedures of the Second Vatican Council and those of the subsequent Synods. At the Council, the participants were accustomed to base their discussions on texts prepared by various commissions, amending them as necessary or even replacing them with different texts. At the Synod, the *Instrumentum Laboris* does not serve as the basis for discussion. Participants are even advised not to refer back to it lest it serve to inhibit new insights and spontaneity.[2]

At the opposite end of the preparation phase, the Synod can be viewed as continuing over a number of months and years. Cooperating with the various permanent offices of the Synod Secretariat, the Holy Father is asked to prepare a final document -- in this instance, the concerns expressed in the forty-three confidential propositions submitted by the bishops to the Holy Father at the end of the Synod as well as the points raised in the Bishops' "Message to Christian Families" (this, too, at the end of the Synod). One has only to recall the time intervening between the end of the general sessions on Evangelization and on Catechesis and the publication of the respective Apostolic Exhortation on these topics to realize the ongoing nature of the work of individual synods.

In treating problems posed by contemporary family life, the participants at the Synod of 1980 took as a necessary point of departure both theology and theological method. And in their interventions, as Cardinal Ratzinger, the Synod's chief relator or reporter observed, a certain opposition between two significant tendencies began to arise. On Monday, October 6, the Cardinal summed up and put in order the contents of the one hundred sixty-one oral and twenty written interventions representing the work of the first week. In order to assist the eleven small discussion groups, divided according to language, Cardinal Ratzinger divided the material into six headings: (1) the method to be used (induction, deduction, or a combination of the two); (2) the situation of the Catholic family in the contemporary world (social, economic, political, cultural); (3) the Sacrament of Matrimony (preparation, rites, indissolubility, divorce, mixed marriages); (4) the duty of transmitting life (*Humanae Vitae,* abortion); (5) the spirituality of family life (prayer, formation of conscience, Catholic education); and (6) the pastoral action toward the family (preparation, direction of family pastoral programs).

In his particularly revealing exposition and synthesis of the general interventions during the first week of the Synod, the Cardinal focused in on the following:

---

[2] Monsignor Philippe Delhaye, "Quelques Thèmes Majeurs Du Synode, 1980," *Esprit et Vie* (January 15, 1981), 2.

Two tendencies have arisen that must not exclude each other, but, which, however express two points of view. The problem is to reconcile these two tendencies so that they complement each other.

There are Fathers who have insisted that the usual formulas not be repeated, as if the doctrine had been made once and for all and closed. They claim that the doctrines must consist only of theological principles, but must be considered in the history of God's people. The criterion for the doctrine must be the sense of faith of God's people, the experience of couples, the work of theologians and philosophers, the progress of human sciences, and the evaluations of the Church's Magisterium. The principal categories of this method are: history (which expresses itself in the signs of the times) and experience (clarified by the sense of the faithful). It follows that the pastoral action, in some way, must precede the doctrinal judgments to which it must lead.

The second tendency claims that the main pastoral duty is to propose the doctrine of the Church, because salvation depends on this, according to Sacred Scripture. The Church must not be overwhelmed by current opinion, as if it were a sociological doctrine, but must prophetically preach the medicine of the Gospel to the ills of the world. The development of doctrine (which is not denied) is actuated only when faith penetrates the life of men and converts them. Many Fathers believe that a thesis can represent a way of composition and reconciliation between the two tendencies: it is a question of the use made of the Church's teaching in men's lives. It is therefore necessary to have a pedagogical method which helps man reach the Gospel, to build bridges to reduce the distance between the Christian vocation and concrete life.[3]

Frequently in the course of the synod, the divergence between these two methodologies -- the "pastoral" and the "doctrinal" -- surfaced and reference was made to conciliar terms such as *sense of faith* and *signs of the times*. Some of the *circuli minores,* or language groups, were of the opinion that more light could be shed on these expressions by returning to the conciliar texts themselves. Thus in the *Dogmatic Constitution on the Church*, we read:

> The holy People of God shares also in Christ's prophetic office: it spreads abroad its living witness to him, especially by a life of faith and love and by offering to God a sacrifice of praise, the fruit of lips praising his name (cf. Heb 13:15). The whole body of the faithful who have an anointing that comes from the holy one (cf. 1 Jn. 2:20 and 27) cannot err in matters of

---

[3] *L'Osservatore Romano* (English edition), October 20, 1980, p. 14.

faith; this particular characteristic which she possesses, she manifests by means of the supernatural sense of the faith of the whole people, when "from the bishops to the 1st member of the faithful laity, she manifests a universal consent in matters of faith and morals. By this sense of the faith, aroused and sustained by the Spirit of truth, and under the *guidance of the sacred magisterium* and faithfully obeying it, the People of God receive not the mere word of men, but truly the word of God (cf. I TH 2:13) and are indefectibly attached to the faith delivered once for all to the saints (cf. Jude 3), penetrate it more deeply as with the right judgment and apply it more fully in daily life (#12).

These notions are clearly the same those found in the chapter devoted by *Lumen Gentium* to the laity (#35). However, in the latter section, the flow of treatment is clearer. Christ's primacy is affirmed in that, in his role as prophet, he announces the truth and witnesses to it. This teaching of Christ is continued by the hierarchy, as already mentioned in *Lumen Gentium* #25. But the Constitution does not want to let it be thought that this prophetic witness only concerns the pastors of the People of God. The entire People of God can be witness of the faith, in accordance with the form of belief and practice which the Magisterium has transmitted in the name of the Lord.

Christ is the great prophet who proclaimed the kingdom of the Father both by the testimony of his life and the power of his word. Until the full manifestation of his glory, he fulfills this prophetic office, not only by the hierarchy who teach in his name and by his power but also by the laity. He accordingly both establishes them as witnesses and provides them with the sense of the faith and the grace of the word (cf. Acts 2:17-18; Apoc 19:10) so that the power of the Gospel may shine out in daily family and social life. They show themselves to be the children of the promise, if, strong in faith and hope, they make the most of the present time (Eph 5:16; Col 4:5), and with patience await the future glory (cf. Rom 8:25). Let them not hide this their hope then, in the depths of their hearts, but rather express it through the structure of their secular lives in continual conversion and in wrestling "against the world rulers of the darkness, against the spiritual forces of iniquity" (Eph 6:12) (#35).

Thus, by means of this faithful reliance on Vatican II, the preliminary conclusions of the Synod (found especially in the discussions taking place in the *circuli minores*) demonstrated how the opposition between the "doctrinal" and "pastoral" methodologies could be overcome. The Constitution on the Church clearly stressed that the Church's teaching, sometimes infallibly, in other instances, substantially, is conserved by the whole Church. There does not exist, on the one hand, a Magisterium cut off from the faithful and, on the other, a merely passive body of the faithful. All live in the Spirit, who recalls to them the words of Christ assisting them in progressively discovering their value in a way that is ever old and at same time ever new.

Yet, the role of the pastors and the faithful is not the same. Pastors have a special charism (*Lumen Gentium*, chapter III), and when the life of the entire body of Christians seems to present a problem regarding a particular point of faith to be believed or lived, it is the function and responsibility of the Magisterium to serve as the final arbiter. As the Synod noted, the Church's doctrine and moral teaching cannot be determined by public opinion, by the number of those who maintain a particular point of view. The disciple of Christ must seek what is true and not the majority opinion. In fact, this is a working principle for any intelligent research, whether philosophical or scientific. All the more is this attitude necessary when it is a question of God's having spoken to reveal Himself. Thus, it would be a mistake to confuse opinion polls and research statistics with the "sense of the faith."

Closely associated with the "sense of the faith," the theme of the "signs of the times" was just as carefully examined by the Synod Fathers. As the Synod did, it is only worthwhile to recall the teaching of Vatican II on the signs of the times: "To carry out such a task, the Church has always had the duty of scrutinizing the signs of the times and of interpreting them in the light of the Gospel" (#4; cf. #11).

When *Gaudium et Spes* calls for the interpretation of these signs in the light of the message of the Gospel, we might well ask why? Could it not be that these signs of the times are ambivalent if not to say even ambiguous? Such a possibility is indeed treated in the Pastoral Constitution:

> This Council, first of all, intends to judge in this light [of faith] those values most highly prized by our contemporaries and to relate them to their divine source. For such values, insofar as they derive from human genius, which is a gift of God, are exceedingly good yet they are often wrenched from their rightful function by the taint in man's heart, and hence stand in need of purification (#11).

In a pastoral letter to the faithful of the Archdiocese of Munich after the close of the Synod, Cardinal Ratzinger, then Archbishop of that See, wrote:

Regarding those matters involved with the signs of the times, the Synod once again observed that the Christian does not exercise a Hegelian way of looking at reality -- by which the ideal morning meditation consists in reading the newspapers in order to perceive where the spirit of the world is to be found. For the Christian, what is at the cutting edge of the spirit of the world is not necessarily at the cutting edge of knowledge and truth because in his perspective of reality history is not simply a journey necessarily leading to the best destination.... In this sense the Synod referred to a concept of St. Augustine: all of history is a conflict between two types of love -- love of God to the point of despising oneself and love of self to the point of despising God. Thus, only education to love can accustom one to balanced discernment of those signs of the times which are the expression of either one or the other of these two kinds of love.[4]

When a few selected interventions at the Synod of 1980, along with some of the reports emanating from the *circuli minores* are studied, the discussion on the "signs of the times" seemingly reflects tendencies in the direction of historicism whose philosophical origins go back to Hegel. Contemporary historicism places a great deal of emphasis on human freedom and on man's role in the formation of institutions and the development of culture. Thus, it could seem reasonable in the context of such historicism to think that man is at liberty to find a new meaning for the conjugal act, for instance, by changing its end or object, even if this alters the very definition of the institution of marriage itself. Historicism views reality as dynamic, as consisting essentially in the process of development rather than in the *form* of what develops or the *end* to which the development is directed. Consequently, those influenced by this mode of thinking tend to shift attention from the eternal to the temporal, from the transcendent reality of God to his immanent presence and concern.

In traditional theological frameworks, there was room for the development of doctrine, but such development was predictable to the extent, at least, that we could be sure a new development would not *contradict* the former teaching. In a theology more influenced by historicism, a dialectical pattern of development of doctrine is often set forth. In a dialectical concept of the development of doctrine, the world to which the Church

---

[4] Cardinal J. Ratzinger, *Le Message du Synod, 1980,* French translation of Letter to Catholics of Munich, December 8, 1980, *Esprit et Vie* (April 30, 1981), 244.

speaks is a *principle co-equal with received tradition* in determining what doctrine is going to be. Because external factors are considered to be so vital, explanations of teachings, such as that on divorce and remarriage or on contraception, are looked for less within specifically Christian sources (such as the teaching of the New Testament on chastity), and much more from outside sources (philosophical systems based on secularistic models, sociology, psychology, and a myriad of other theories to which orthodox Christianity is seen as constantly "reacting").

Because the historical situation of our day is so very different from that of earlier centuries, it is alleged that a completely new and unexpected teaching can be promulgated by the Church, though never suddenly,[5] even though it be incompatible with the one previously taught and lived by. In fact, from the point of view of historicism, the Church is true to itself only by reacting in this way. The tradition of the Church indeed remains constant, but it must combine with the different situations in which it finds itself to form an entirely new synthesis. It is as though the Church's tradition were a chemical element on the ever increasing periodic table, which can be combined with various other elements. Depending upon the combination which happens to occur at any given time, diverse compounds (doctrines) are formed, and these may have essentially diverse, even contrary, properties.

One illustration of the prevalence of the foregoing attitudes may be gleaned from what follows. Reporting on the 1980 Bishops' Synod, the editor of the *East Asian Pastoral Review* observed:

> Last October the Synod on the Family ended without much press coverage. The problems were many and the expectations few, since the solutions presented by the "traditional doctrine" had been repeatedly reaffirmed by high instances of the Church; the outcome was known in advance....
>
> Some insisted on inculturation. A controversial item was the concept of "dynamic progressive marriage" (customary marriages), which some eighteen bishops asked to be considered as possible, since, according to one bishop it is not contrary to the Gospel. Cardinal Knox, Prefect of the Congregation of Sacraments and Divine Worship, condemned outrightly such "lewd and pernicious concubinage"; this sparked a swift reaction which dubbed his eminence's ideas as "theological neocolonialism...."

---

[5] Bernard Häring, C.SS.R., "The Synod of Bishops and the Family: Pastoral Reflections," *Studia Moralia* 19 (1981): 239.

If "progressive marriage" did not rally the Synod's enthusiasm, the general principle of inculturation was heartily approved, with the note that the local bishops may decide what is or is not "Catholic." This can be a far-reaching decision if Rome allows it to blossom.... This concept ("pastoral mercy") might perhaps be the best fruit of the Synod, if it is not frozen into a canon or "explained" by the "authentic" magisterium ... "Pastoral mercy" draws its promising usefulness from its vagueness. The same could be said of the "principle of gradualism." As long as it is left undetermined, even ambiguous, the local Churches will apply it to such different mentalities and degrees of moral development as are to be found in Latin America, Papua New Guinea, Africa, not to mention the neo-pagans of the "first world." But, if it is expounded with Cartesian clarity and distinctiveness, it runs the risk of becoming a purely formal principle, good for textbooks but unavailing for practical life....

The result of the Synod is crystallized in 43 (secret) propositions, handed over to the pope. As they stand, they are not impressive, indeed. Drafted in a culinary Latin -- with grammatical errors, to boot -- they display assorted ideas on the family, in a tormented style, the fruit of a piecemeal composition, which renders the meaning always difficult, at times unintelligible. They attempt to systematize the contents into three parts, appending an annex asking for a charter of rights and a pastoral directory. The first part deals with general principles: the sense of faith, signs of the times and gradualism. The second presents the theology of Matrimony and the third, the pastoral questions. But the ideas are mixed up and often anarchically distributed, as if some *modi* would have each paragraph say everything.[6]

With reference to this "ideal" interpretation of the "law of gradualism," which was treated by the editor of the *East Asian Pastoral Review,* Pope John Paul II, in his concluding address to the Synod of Bishops, stated:

> Directing their attention to those things which concern pastoral ministry for the good of spouses and of families, the Fathers of the Synod rejected any type of division or "dichotomy" between a pedagogy, which takes into account a certain progression in accepting the plan of God, and doctrine, proposed by the Church, with all its consequences, in which the precept of living according to the same doctrine is contained; in which case there is not a question of a desire of keeping the law as merely an ideal to be

---

[6] Editorial, "The Bishops' Synod, 1980," *East Asian Pastoral Review* (January 1981), 4-5.

achieved in the future but rather of the mandate of Christ the Lord that difficulties constantly be overcome. Really, the "process of gradualness," as it is called, cannot be applied unless someone accepts divine law with a sincere heart and seeks those goods which are protected and promoted by the same law.[7]

The sentiments expressed in the *East Asian Pastoral Review* even before the promulgation of the Apostolic Exhortation, *Familiaris Consortio,* are quite similar to a number of those which were expressed, both in the popular press and even in some professional journals by certain theologians and others, almost immediately after its publication in this country. A number of these reactions ran as follows:

Peter Hebblethwaite (*National Catholic Reporter*, 1 Jan. 1982, p. 12):

> John Paul responded to the majority view at the synod. One cannot complain that he did not listen to them. But the minority view was first caricatured, then processed out, and finally dismissed with arguments of questionable validity. The vanquished can console themselves with John Paul's remarks that "the Church seeks the truth, which is not always the same as the majority opinion."
>
> Although *Familiaris Consortio* follows the main outlines of the synod propositions, it could have been written even if the synod had never met. It contains twenty-four quotations from Pope John Paul's addresses delivered before the synod met. The truth is he is an expert on the subject of marriage and the family, and so he did not need the synod's advice on these matters.
>
> But before one concludes that the synod was an expensive waste of time, one should consider the possibility that its function has changed: instead of giving advice to someone who does not need it, it becomes a celebration of the unity of the bishops gathered around the pope. It was indeed a famous victory. Time will tell whether it was a Pyrrhic victory.

Fr. Richard McBrien (*Washington Post*, 16 Dec. 1981, p. A18):

> I don't suspect it is going to change anybody's mind one way or another. Catholics today have learned what it means to be selectively obedient to the Church's teachings.

---

[7] *L'Osservatore Romano* (English edition) (November 3, 1980), p. 6.

Fr. Andrew Greeley (*L.A. Herald Examiner*, 16 Jan. 1982, p. B8):

There are really two different kinds of religion: the kind that thinks God talks to human kind only through religious leaders, and the kind that thinks God's spirit (or God's Spirit, if you will) speaks also through ordinary people. ...
... the long document shows little effect of any lay contribution. Indeed, the synod of the bishops on the family, which the pope was summarizing in his exhortation, had only a few carefully selected lay people around as "observers." However fine the pope's notion of lay contribution may be in theory, the Catholic Church is organized in such a way that they cannot make that contribution in practice.
Nor are the power-hungry barons of the Roman Curia likely to give them a chance – ever, if they can help it.
So you have the ludicrous spectacle of a group of elderly unmarried men pontificating easily and freely about the problems of marriage, sex, and family life without any need to listen to those who are married, have families, and experience sexual intimacy.

Dr. David Thomas (*National Catholic Reporter*, 15 Jan. 1982, p. 19):

Now that I have had the opportunity to read through the document – with intensity and interest almost as great as I experience in reading my wife's letters before we were married – I come away feeling both delighted and depressed. What delighted me most was the outright affirmation that the Christian family is indeed church in a radical decisive way – and that the rest of the Church is best described in family terms. What depressed me is the same matter that bothered me at the synod itself – little advance is made in formulating a practical, experientially rooted theology of marriage and the family. Such a theology is needed – and I would add already available – yet the church does not seem to be ready or equipped to look for that treasure.

Fr. John Finnegan (*Milwaukee Sentinel*, 16 Jan. 1982, p. 5, part I):

Divorced and remarried Catholics can still receive the sacraments under special circumstances without annulments even though Pope John Paul recently reaffirmed the church's stand against such a procedure.
This was the opinion of Fr. John Finnegan, past president of the Canon Law Society of America. Finnegan, a Boston inner city pastor who has specialized in divorce ministry for 20 years, gave a workshop on divorce ministry to area priests Friday at Catholic Family Ministry. The workshop was closed to the press.

In an interview, Finnegan discussed the implications of the section on divorce in the pope's document on family issues. While he disagreed with the section on divorce, Finnegan said he thought it was a superb encyclical that made a serious attempt to give a "spirituality of marriage."

Finnegan, a marriage tribunal judge for the Boston Archdiocese, said for hundreds of years there has been a tradition in the church where confessors can reconcile people to the Church through the internal forum

... In his encyclical, the pope said the only way divorced people who remarried outside the Church could receive the sacraments was to live in "complete continence" abstaining from conjugal acts.

"I'm disappointed in that portion of the papal statement ... the brother-sister solution was always humanly inadequate," Finnegan said. "I always felt that it could only be invented by celibates."

Finnegan indicated the Pope's statement on divorce would have little impact on the majority of divorced Catholics in the United States because it would be ignored.

"*I prefer to see Catholics* ... cull all the good out of this encyclical that is there for them ... and *be able to lay aside those sections that they feel are inappropriate for their own lives,*" he said.

"I used to tell my students that I never disobey a church law ... I do dispense myself from church law at times," he said.

Fr. Henry Sattler (*National Catholic Register*, 14 Nov. 1982, p. 5):

The "National Consultation on *Familiaris Consortio*" was held at the Theological College at Catholic University of America, Washington, D.C., Sept. 11-13, 1982. The consultation was presented by the National Institute on the Family, a spin-off organization from the USCC's Family Life Desk, directed by Father Donald Conroy, the former National Family Life Director at USCC. The assembly of about 150 people was comprised mostly of laity with a sprinkling of clergy and religious. The group was addressed by Bishop J. Francis Stafford, the chief representative of the American hierarchy at the Synod of 1980, and by some 25 other speakers.

The meeting turned out to be no consultation at all. The members were not asked to consult or witness but to become an audience for the lectures of the presenters. With some exceptions, the brief presentations were either dissenting or non-committal. Those rising from the floor were permitted to ask questions, but when making positive suggestions were placed in the position of being dissenters from what was being said from the podium rather than supporters of the insight of *Familiaris Consortio*.

A request from one gentleman from the floor to be enabled to take home and make understandable the insights of John Paul instead of just those of objectors was greeted with mere silence by that panel. More than a few couples present were very positive toward *Familiaris Consortio* but did not speak up in what seemed to them a hostile atmosphere. A suggestion from the floor asked that the papal exhortation be given sympathetic time and explanation at least equal to that of the objectors was ignored and subsequent attempts to support the document were dismissed.

The first positive and approving presentation of the doctrinal content of *Familiaris Consortio* was given by Archbishop Hickey of Washington, D.C., and he was not on the program to speak. He motioned those at the liturgy to be seated after the Post-Communion Prayer and spoke without introduction. His intervention was a nice antidote to the majority of the other speakers. After Archbishop Hickey spoke, the tone of the remaining presentations became more bland, especially during the presentations on pastoral practice and on apostolic activity. However, this blandness does not show up in the written work prepared beforehand by a number of the speakers.

Again and again it appeared that a number of the presenters objected to and rejected what they said was an erroneous ecclesiology of John Paul II. Repeatedly, they seemed to be saying that the Church is composed of both laity and hierarchy who have equal authority to the extent that one can determine the content of faith by the (con)*sensus fidelium*. John Paul II, with Vatican II, insists that though the insight of all the faithful (a *sensus fidei* – the supernatural sense of the faith) is to be taken into account as a theological source, the final judgment and certification of truth lies with the hierarchy (*Familiaris Consortio*, 2; *Lumen Gentium*, 12, 25; *Mysterium Ecclesiae*, 2).

It was severally denied by the speakers that celibacy and virginity are charisms superior to that of marriage. This is a direct contradiction of John Paul: "... the Church throughout her history has always defended the superiority of this charism to that of marriage, by reason of the wholly singular link which it has with the kingdom of God ..." (#42).

There were some very good presentations, notably those of the several made by couples, especially by the couple who spoke (unscheduled and hastily requested to do so) of their positive experience as auditors at the Synod. The brief analysis of the proposed new Code on Marriage was excellent. The summations in the last session were good or at least conciliatory to the teaching on *Familiaris Consortio*.

It seemed, however, that most of the speakers took diametrically opposite positions to *Familiaris Consortio* in the areas of contraception, indissolubility, the sacramentality of matrimony, the right to the Eucharist for the divorced and "remarried," the superiority of celibacy and virginity over matrimony, ecclesiology, the sensus fidei as a theological "locus," inculturation, the right of the Magisterium to teach authoritatively, the evil of marital coitus exclusively for pleasure, etc.

All in all it seemed to this observer that the consultation planted the seeds for dissent from the beautifully positive teaching of John Paul II in his exhortation, which responded to every proposition of the Synod, though perhaps not n the way some persons expected.

These sentiments fall into the category of what the distinguished Swiss theologian, Father Hans Urs von Balthasar, has termed the anti-Roman attitude, which deep-seated attitude the Church community must overcome. Thus he writes:

> It is commonly said, "You cannot trust Rome," meaning that Rome will always be the same: she wants to rule, and she misuses the supreme authority given her for service to impose legalistic obedience on the people. Hence her adherents regress with her from evangelical freedom to the alienating religion of the Law, the old Covenant. Newman, in his early, still-Anglican work, "The Prophetic Office of the Church," strongly expresses this lack of trust....
>
> Does not the young Newman here give a summary of the objection of the anti-Roman attitude against the "system" which stands like the Great Wall of China, hard and impenetrable, between the soul and God, between the believer and the living Christ of the Gospel? And even if the Christian could find, as in a code or hieroglyph, the original living meaning of God's communication, the Roman form achieves merely an unnecessary distancing. Mediation offered is of no use; it invites contradiction.
>
> As it happened, Newman learned better when he became acquainted with the Catholic saints and the Fathers of the undivided Church. He found not alienation but a blessed intimacy with God and self, guarded in faith and in love by the unifying power of the Church. The Church's minimal demands to the lukewarm and the mediocre are all open-ended and are meant to stimulate free spontaneity. And while a demand of the Gospel professed only in books can -- and frequently does -- leave us mired in sloth, what comes to us from the living authority of the Church challenges us unremittingly. Even if it does not affect us in practice, just knowing that in the midst of what is happening now in the world there is such a living, guiding, and goading center does not permit us to remain indifferent. And if we listen to her, she gives us a sublime, soaring certainty that we are not straying from the right path and are not subject to the risks and dangers that threaten lonely seekers.[8]

---

[8] Hans Urs von Balthasar, "The Anti-Roman Attitude," translated by Andrèe Emery, *Communio* 8 (Winter 1981): 313-14.

The Apostolic Exhortation *Familiaris Consortio* continues to assist those preparing for marriage in that listening, and serves to provide that certainty especially to those Christian families who before the promulgation of this Apostolic Exhortation regarding the role of the Christian family, may indeed have considered themselves often lonely and even foolish seekers after the Church's cherished ideals of Christian family life.

Chapter Three

Reflections on Salesian Anthropology [1]

Rev. JOHN W. CROSSIN, O.S.F.S.

As we honor the work of John F. Harvey, O.S.F.S., I would like to reflect in particular on the human person, made in the image of God, and thus made to relate deeply to others. For over fifty years, Father Harvey has engaged in effective pastoral relationships with others. He has manifested the virtue of love in serving others. A reflection on human identity and relationality seems very appropriate in the context of honoring him.

Father Harvey is an extraordinarily gregarious person. He has many friends, colleagues and admirers. He has provided instruction, counseling and spiritual guidance for numerous groups and individuals over the many years of his ministry.

Not only is Father Harvey skilled in personal relationships, but his professional writings and work show a strong emphasis on relationships. The *Courage* movement which Father and his friends founded in 1980 stresses group support and spiritual friendship for people with homosex-

---

[1] I wish to thank Very Rev. Joseph Morrissey, O.S.F.S., Provincial Superior of the Oblates of St. Francis de Sales for his generosity in providing the sabbatical year during which this essay was written. Likewise, I would like to thank Rev. James Connor, S.J., Director of the Woodstock Theological Center at Georgetown University and Rev. Joseph Tylenda, S.J., Woodstock Librarian, for their gracious hospitality during my year as a Visiting Fellow.

ual inclinations.[2] In his book, *The Homosexual Person*, Father Harvey discusses at some length the theory of Elizabeth Moberly that stresses the relational origins of homosexuality.[3] After examining his writings and observing his teaching, I think it fair to say that a focus on positive human relationships is a consistent emphasis with Father Harvey.

This relational emphasis certainly is rooted in his deep love and reverence for St. Francis de Sales (1567-1622) and his teaching. The remainder of this essay will explore some aspects of the teaching of De Sales on relationships and some contemporary developments that I believe are consonant with this teaching. This discussion will, I hope, not only illumine some of the anthropological roots of Father Harvey's work but also develop the foundations for my own efforts to elaborate a contemporary Salesian virtue ethics.[4]

Bases of Salesian Anthropology

As many theologians do today, St. Francis de Sales begins his considerations, for example in his *Treatise on the Love of God*,[5] with the human person.[6] De Sales begins with the Greek axiom: "Know

---

[2] See John F. Harvey, O.S.F.S., *The Homosexual Person: New Thinking in Pastoral Care* (San Francisco: Ignatius Press, 1987), 119-74, and *The Truth About Homosexuality: The Cry of the Faithful* (San Francisco: Ignatius Press, 1996), 19-30.

[3] See *The Homosexual Person*, 38-48.

[4] See my *Friendship: The Key to Spiritual Growth* (New York: Paulist, 1997) and *Walking in Virtue: Moral Decisions and Spiritual Growth in Daily Life* (New York: Paulist, 1998).

[5] St. Francis de Sales, *Treatise on the Love of God*, trans. with and introduction and notes by John K. Ryan, 2 vols. (Rockford, IL: TAN, 1974).

[6] See Lewis S. Fiorelli, "Salesian Understanding of Christian Anthropology," *Salesianum* 46 (1984): 487-508 for a detailed and lucid discussion of Salesian anthropology. For a comprehensive view of the human person as loving God and neighbor, see James S. Langelaan, *The Philosophy and Theology of Love According to St. Francis de Sales*, Toronto Studies in Theology, vol. 67 (Lewiston, NY: Edwin Mellen Press, 1992).

Thyself."[7] This knowledge of self is attained primarily in going out of oneself and reflecting on this experience and not predominately in introspection.[8] Thus, in acting we come to know ourselves. And action brings us into contact with others.[9]

This Christian examination of the person who goes out of self to others led St. Francis to the mystery of our creation in the divine image. De Sales' conception of the human person and his spirituality is rooted here. Reflection on this divine image leads to a consideration of the Giver and thus to the Trinity. Likewise, it leads to a consideration of our human relationships with one another. We will consider the Trinity initially and our relationships with one another later in this essay.

The Trinity

> For all eternity there is in God an essential communication by which the Father, in producing the Son, communicates his entire infinite and indivisible divinity as the Son. The Father and the Son together, in producing the Holy Spirit, communicate in like manner their own proper unique divinity to him.[10]

---

[7] We should note that knowledge of self comes in dialogue with others as well as in introspection. We come to know ourselves over the course of a lifetime. This growth in self-knowledge is part of our spiritual and moral development. I believe this development is part of the growth in the virtue of love delineated by De Sales in his *Treatise*.

[8] Fiorelli, 488.

[9] A fruitful development of Salesian thought might occur in dialogue with Pope John Paul II's reflections on the "Acting Person." De Sales sees the human person as made to go out of self to others. He speaks in his *Treatise* of the "ecstasy of action." The Pope's phenomenological-thomistic reflections could make for a fruitful development of this aspect of Salesian spirituality. I will not be able to pursue this line of inquiry here. See Rocco Buttiglione, *Karol Wojtyla: The Thought of the Man Who Became Pope John Paul II*, trans. Paolo Guietti and Francesca Murphy (Grand Rapids, MI: Wm. B. Eerdmans, 1997), 117-77.

[10] St. Francis de Sales, *Treatise*, I:11.

For De Sales, this communicative essence of God appropriately, but not by necessity, expresses itself in the creation of the universe and of the human person. God's inner life of love is ecstatic. It very appropriately expresses itself in creation.

A contemporary author, Mary Timothy Prokes, develops an emphasis similar to that of De Sales when she notes:

> To be human is to be created in the image of God and the call to human mutuality can be recognized in the divine paradigm where 1) the *identity* of each divine person is in *relation* to the other two; 2) their perfect mutual love requires a *third*; 3) their reciprocal love is an *indwelling*; and 4) the basis of their interrelationship is *personal self-gift*.[11]

There is a *"perfect reciprocal giving and receiving among Trinitarian Persons."*[12] This inclination toward mutuality is present in human persons as made in God's image.

Norris Clarke goes a step beyond Prokes and speaks of the receptivity of the divine persons.

> For just as the Father's whole personality as Father consists in his communicating, *giving,* the entire divine nature that is his own to the Son, his eternal Word, so reciprocally the Son's whole personality as Son consists in *receiving*, eternally and fully, with loving gratitude, this identical divine nature from his Father. The Son, as distinct from the Father, is subsistent Receiver, so to speak.[13]

There is no imperfection in this communication. And we, as mutual communicators in God's image, might be seen to have a certain receptivity to others since we are made in the divine image.

---

[11] *Mutuality: The Human Image of Trinitarian Love* (New York: Paulist Press, 1993), 34.

[12] *Mutuality*, 7.

[13] Norris Clarke, S.J., "Reply to Steven Long," *The Thomist* 61 (1997): 618.

Made in God's Image[14]

The human person is made in the image of this creative, loving and "receptive" God. Of what does this image consist? Primarily for De Sales it consists in loving; but it is not limited to loving. In his *Spiritual Conferences*,[15] St. Francis stresses that we are like God in being reasonable; in his *Treatise on the Love of God*, we are like God in loving. Yet, St. Francis' view is even more wide ranging.

> We are created to the image and likeness of God.... Our soul is spiritual, indivisible, and immortal. It understands, it wills, and it wills freely. It is capable of judging, of reasoning, of knowing and of having virtues. In all this, it resembles God.[16]

Most characteristically, De Sales believes *the image of the triune God in the human person is in loving*. This human love is ecstatic; that is, it goes outside of itself. In so doing, it can follow two paths. The person can degrade him or herself and become like the animals or can rise above self and become devout. Our love can be self-less or self-centered.[17]

The loving image in Salesian thinking embraces an appropriate self-love. For "we should love ourselves—not in an inordinate sense of self-love, but because we are reflections of the Trinity...."[18] In humility, we accept the being and the talents that God has given us. All we are is a gift from a loving Triune God.

---

[14] Most of this section and some of the subsequent reflections are drawn from John W. Crossin, O.S.F.S. "Salesian Spirituality and Adult Developmental Psychology" (Ph.D. diss., The Catholic University of America, 1982), chap. 2.

[15] These were given over the years to the Sisters of the Visitation. For an English translation, see *The Spiritual Conferences of St. Francis de Sales*, trans. by Albert Gasquet and Canon H.B. Mackey O.S.B. (Westminster, MD: Newman Press, 1962), Conference 3.

[16] *Treatise*, I: 91.

[17] See Fiorelli, 496.

[18] Cornelius Kilty, O.S.F.S., "Aspects of Salesian Anthropology" (M.A. thesis, De Sales School of Theology, 1970), 29.

In striving to be self-less, the human person exercises human freedom. He or she seeks to act responsibly. In this freedom too, the person is the reflection of God. Though wounded by sin, the person can still wish to love God above all things and, with the help of grace, can actually freely fulfill this desire by a movement of love toward God.[19]

Human Sinfulness

The person made in the image of God has sinned—'originally' through Adam and Eve. De Sales sees the effects of sin as profound. Our wills, in which lies our ability to love, are greatly weakened by sin. Our intellects are less severely though quite obviously affected. We can see that God is worthy of love, but we are unable to love Him. The damage of sin reverberates throughout our whole being. Yet

> ... that holy inclination to love God above all things remains with us, as does the natural light of reason by which we know that his supreme goodness is loveable above all things. It is impossible for a man who thinks attentively about God, even by natural reason alone, not to feel a certain glow of love.[20]

The human link to God is not completely severed. Even apart from grace, the human person can have a certain wish to love God above all things. Such wishes can never be fulfilled by human efforts alone: "Only after God has revealed himself as man's final fulfillment does there arise in man the desire to be united with him, 'desire' meaning here a movement of love by which man aims at possessing the desired object."[21]

We might elaborate quite briefly on De Sales' thought in noting that today we often look at sin in terms of the rupture of relationships—with

---

[19] See Crossin, "Salesian Spirituality and Adult Developmental Psychology," 62-66, for more on human sinfulness and God's grace; also see Fiorelli, 498-99, 504-06.

[20] *Treatise*, I: 94.

[21] James S. Langelaan, O.S.F.S., "Man, the Image and Likeness of God: Nature and Supernature according to St. Francis de Sales," *Downside Review* 95 (1977): 45.

our neighbor, with our community and with God.[22] Contemporary authors note that our relationships affect us at an early age. Thus, we learn certain ways of thinking and acting. Our moral sense seems to develop in our relationships with others.[23] Similarly, our emotional reactions are formed in our early relationships.[24] If these relationships are characterized by the "negativities" of sinful humanity—such as abuse, exploitation, and violence—we can spend our adult lives seeking to compensate for the impact of this sin in our lives. Likewise, even in our adult lives, we can see the impact of sinful relationships on us. Others can lead us away from God. A clear example of this is the drug gang that leads its members to violence and self-destruction.

Today, theologians also speak of the structures of sin. We humans are very much affected by the communal and organizational structures which permeate our daily lives. Thus, for example, an unjust economic system can lead people to live in poverty and to steal from others in order to survive; oppressive and corrupt governmental structures can encourage drug dealing and violence. Such social structures can lead the human person astray just as more positive structures which respect human dignity and encourage human development can help form the person for the good.[25]

---

[22] For a brief discussion of the traditional criteria for judging human acts and of moral discernment, see my *Walking in Virtue*, chapter six.

[23] See James Q. Wilson, *The Moral Sense* (New York: The Free Press, 1993) for a lengthy discussion, from a social scientific and biological point of view, of our early moral development. Wilson says: "To anticipate and oversimplify the conclusion, it is that an older view of human nature than is now current in the human sciences and moral philosophy is the correct view. Thinking seriously about the kinds of animals we are will help us understand our persistent but fragile disposition to make moral judgments and the aspects of human relations that must be cultivated if that disposition is to be protected and nurtured" (p. xv).

[24] For an in-depth discussion of this question, see G. Simon Harak, S.J., *Virtuous Passions: The Formation of Christian Character* (New York: Paulist Press, 1993).

[25] See Bernard J.F. Lonergan, S.J., *A Third Collection*, ed. Frederick E. Crowe, S.J. (New York: Paulist; London: Geoffrey Chapman, 1985), 9-10, where he notes the necessity of a good community for authentic living.

The Grace of Jesus Christ

Salesian thought, reflecting Christian conviction, holds that human sinfulness is healed only through the grace of Jesus Christ. God's gracious love is given to humanity in Jesus. Our relationships with God and others as well as our own interior lives are healed by the grace of the Holy Spirit. God communicates with humanity in His Son and continues this communication in the sacraments and especially in the Eucharist. God's grace forms a loving community, which is the Church.

As we elaborate on De Sales' ideas, we would note the power of grace to heal the hurts and broken relationships of life. We also should insist that, just as with growth in virtue in De Sales, this healing takes time and perhaps a lifetime.[26]

Christ's Spirit can heal unjust communal and social structures as well as individual sinfulness, but this requires much human cooperation with grace just as personal healing does.[27] It takes great effort to create, build and perpetuate the positive social structures that make for justice and human development. As noted at the Second Vatican Council, the Church itself is in need of constant reform. Sinfulness affects its members and structures just as it affects those in secular society.

Friendship and Community

If others can pull us down, they can also help us to grow in the divine image—in proper self-love, in freedom, and in love for God. People need friendships with others to grow in the divine image.

---

[26] See my "When Relationships Falter: Sin, Healing and Reconciliation," in *Friendship*, chapter 7. See also John Farrelly, O.S.B., "St. Francis de Sales and Modern Historical Consciousness," in *Salesian Spirituality: Catalyst to Collaboration*, ed. William J. Ruhl, O.S.F.S. (Washington, D.C.: DeSales School of Theology, 1993), 162-65; Jon Sobrino, "Liberation from Sin," *Theology Digest* 37/2 (Summer 1990): 141-45 and Jurgen Moltmann, "The Theology of Our Liberation," Theology *Digest* 45/1 (Spring 1998): 3-5.

[27] For a brief reflection on the virtue of justice, see my *What Are They Saying About Virtue?* (New York: Paulist Press, 1985), 32-35. Also see Josef Pieper, *The Four Cardinal Virtues* (Notre Dame: University of Notre Dame Press, 1966), 43-113, for a discussion of justice by a leading contemporary Thomist.

Solidarity with all people, who also image the triune God, effects our outward ecstasy to the neighbor as well. Francis brought this out in a sermon (October 4, 1614): "Man has been created to the resemblance of God; therefore, love of the neighbor leads us to love in him the resemblance and image of God, that is to say (that we are to help) to render this resemblance more and more perfect."[28]

Mutual relationships are most important for our spiritual growth.[29] There is in us both a need to go out to others and a receptivity to others. Of course, our giving and receiving is a faint image of the Trinity.

Furthermore, being in the living image of God, the person is oriented to others and thus toward community. John O'Donnell puts it well when he writes: "From a theological perspective, the deepest reason for the human being's sociality is that the person is created in the image of the Trinity, the perfect community, where the three divine persons exist in an eternal self-giving."[30] There is in us a need to be in giving relationships with others. Loving relationships make for our spiritual growth. These loving relationships make a community. There is a reciprocal effect in relationships that can encourage spiritual growth and build a Christian community. Ideally, the loving image of God comes to fruition in the Church.

> The Trinitarian paradigm applies to the whole people of God, in both universal ecclesial life and in multiple local communities. In order to appreciate the challenges inherent in such an expectation, it is important to enumerate...the qualities of perichoretic [Trinitarian] love: 1) mutual self-gift; 2) mutual deference; 3) accord in act and will; 4) co-presence in the missions of other persons; and 5) mutual indwelling. Jesus describes perichoretic relations as total self-donation and total receptivity without domination or self-aggrandizement. This is beyond perfect fulfillment for Christians living in a sin-wounded world, but it is always a matter of fruitful tension between the "already" and the "not yet." Immersed in history, communities of faith, like individuals, must move honestly through stages of development. It is not surprising, then, that the church experi-

---

[28] Fiorelli, 501.

[29] Prokes offers an extended discussion of mutuality in her Chapter Three, "The Human Search for Mutuality," 38-62.

[30] as cited in Prokes, 36.

ences "spasms" of difficulty in attempting to realize perichoretic relations. Within the abiding church, each generation, each culture, each era of human development progresses through unique times of growth, blockage and breakthrough.[31]

Our constant effort to build a community of love flows from our imaging of God who is love. Our always-deficient efforts reflect our sinfulness yet triumph with the help of God's grace.

Relationship with God

There is in us an active receptivity to others in community. Likewise, there is a receptivity to a relationship with God. In a human relationship with God, however, a certain dissimilarity predominates. Alexander Pocetto believes that "The most original aspect of Salesian thought on the affinity between God and man does not rest on the principles of similarity but rather on the notion of dissimilarity."[32] There is a correspondence between God and the human person. Our indigence can be filled by God's bountifulness.

> In addition to this congruity based on likeness, there is an unparalleled correspondence between God and man because of their reciprocal perfection. This does not mean that God can receive any perfection from man. But just as man cannot be perfected except by the divine goodness, so also divine goodness can rightly exercise its perfection outside itself nowhere so well as upon our humanity.[33]

St. Francis sees the human person both as made in the image of God and having a deep correspondence with God. This orientation is inborn and is strengthened through the grace of the Holy Spirit.

---

[31] Prokes, 82-83. Her entire Chapter Four, "The Church as Sacrament of Trinitarian Mutuality" (pp. 63-105), makes for interesting and thought-provoking reading.

[32] Alexander T. Pocetto, "An Introduction to Salesian Anthropology," *Salesian Studies* 6(Summer, 1969): 48.

[33] Francis de Sales, *Treatise*, 1: 91.

In Salesian thought, the main other to whom the human person is oriented is Christ, for "the mighty Savior was first in God's intention and in that eternal plan which divine providence formed for the production of creatures."[34] Christ is the Alpha and the Omega. All creation came into being in light of His coming and all creation will be completed in Him. Jesus is the ultimate goal who gives purpose to all creation. Human fulfillment is in Christ. God's love is so great that he sent Christ so that we might be united with Him in glory. Fiorelli summarizes this in saying, "The human family, along with all else, was made with special reference to the humanity of the Logos, Jesus Christ. The Second Person of the Trinity is not only the vehicle, as Word, for creation. He is also the reason for creation. Thus, one element of Salesian anthropology is certainly the Christo-centricity of the human person."[35] The person is made for fulfillment in Christ. This is, of course, a fulfillment in loving.

Prokes adds further to our understanding of the centrality of Christ when she says:

> Jesus Christ is the bonding point, the enduring expression of total self-gift, the embodied realization of divine-human giving and receiving. In his visible earthly life, Jesus consistently brought persons and things into fruitful relationship.... He opened his followers to the unguessed potential for synergistic union within the simplest of earthly beings and actions. To be human is to be called to perichoretic self-gift, in and through the body. As Jesus knew and experienced, this means a willingness to suffer the forgetfulness, selfishness, treachery and betrayal of others.[36]

We can only attain our fullest humanity in Christ. The Gospel is not extrinsic to us but fulfills our deepest longings. God desires that we be joined to Him, but we are free to choose otherwise. Despite the human choice of sin, God still loves us and desires to be united with us.

We might sum up by saying that De Sales' theology of love therefore sees the Trinity, Creation, the Human Person, the Incarnation and Redemption intrinsically linked together. All these are mysteries of love.

---

[34] *Treatise*, I:114.

[35] Fiorelli, 493.

[36] Prokes, 141–42.

Philosophical Reflections

These extended (but far from exhaustive) theological reflections on the human person as created in the divine image, that is, in the image of the Trinity, can lead us to consider whether there might also be a philosophical basis for the Salesian focus on relationships. W. Norris Clarke, S.J., Emeritus Professor of Philosophy at Fordham University, offers a congenial and compelling philosophical approach which complements and expands the foregoing analysis.[37] He offers an approach that is contemporary, Thomistic, and relational.[38]

> My defense of this position is quite explicitly an exercise in "Christian philosophy," that is, using the Christian revelation of the Trinity (one God in three Persons) as a principle of *Illumination* (not rigorous, purely philosophical argument) to shed new light on the deeper meaning of both person and being, helping us to notice more positive aspects of both even in our own world that may have escaped our attention so far. This kind of specifically Christian philosophizing has been practiced very fruitfully in recent years in this country by Christian thinkers....[39]

With this Christian sensitivity, Clarke then proceeds to examine St. Thomas Aquinas' metaphysics once more to look for a properly philosophical justification for a dynamic human relationality.

---

[37] See Norris Clarke, S.J., *Person and Being* (Milwaukee: Marquette University, 1993); his "Person, Being and St. Thomas," *Communio* 19 (Winter 1992): 601-18 and his *Explorations in Metaphysics: Being—God—Person* (Notre Dame: University of Notre Dame, 1994). Clarke's views have provoked considerable discussion. See David Schindler in *Communio* 20 (Fall 1993): 580-98; Steven Long, George Blair, David Schindler, and Norris Clarke in *Communio* 21(Spring 1994): 151-90; Steven Long, "Personal Receptivity and Act: A Thomistic Critique," *The Thomist* 61/1 (1997): 1-31; and Norris Clarke, "A Reply to Steven Long," *The Thomist* 61/4 (1997):617-24. Schindler supports the basic thrust of Clarke's work, while Long and Blair are critical of Clarke's ideas.

[38] For a short overview of contemporary Thomistic approaches, see Gerald McCool, "The Tradition of St. Thomas since Vatican II," *Theology Digest* 40/4 (1993): 324-35. McCool consider Clarke to be a personalist Thomist and groups him with Karol Wojtyla (Pope John Paul II).

[39] Norris Clarke, "A Reply to Steven Long," 618.

Clarke considers his work a "creative retrieval and completion of Aquinas view on the metaphysics of the human person."[40] He begins to draw out a dynamic and relational notion of the human person that is not explicit but below the surface in Aquinas. Our existential being is act and is "intrinsically ordered toward self-communication."[41]

As is well known, relationality is a strong emphasis in contemporary philosophy and in contemporary psychology and culture. However, in this emphasis, the metaphysical notion of substance tends to disappear. That is, for some the person does not even exist if not in relationship. According to Clarke, Aquinas offers a balance: "... the being of the person has been explained as one-sidedly in terms of relation and systems of relations that the dimension of the person as abiding self-identity, interiority, and in-itselfness has tended to disappear from sight, or at least lose all metaphysical grounding."[42]

For Clarke there is in the person an indissoluble complementarity of substantiality and relationality. Clarke hopes to:

> make a start on this integration by grafting the self-communicative, relational dimension of the person right onto the Thomistic metaphysics of being as existential, self-communicative act, showing how it is already in principle implicit therein. I propose to do this by developing the dynamic, relational aspect of being itself for St. Thomas, with its indissoluble complementarity of substantiality, the *in-itself* dimension of being, and relationality, the *toward-others* aspect.[43]

Clarke goes on to develop his justification and elaborate this inseparability at some length. He contends that "There must be an *in-itself* somewhere along the line to ground the betweeness. This is the ontological role of substance in a being: to provide the abiding unifying center for all the being's relations and other attributes."[44] Being is

---

[40] *Person and Being*, 1.

[41] *Person and Being*, 3.

[42] *Person and Being*, 4-5.

[43] *Person and Being*, 5.

[44] *Person and Being*, 16.

likewise intrinsically active and self-communicating. Relationality is thus primordial in Aquinas.

> The innate dynamism of being as overflowing into self-manifesting, self-communicating action is clear and explicit in St. Thomas, if one knows where to look. Not as explicit, however, though necessarily implied, it seems to me, is the corollary that *relationality* is a primordial dimension of every real being, inseparable from its substantiality, just as action is from existence. For if a being naturally flows over into self-communicating action toward others, and receives from them, then it cannot help but generate a network of relations with all its recipients.[45]

And this network of relations leads to community: "... real being, as intrinsically self-communication and relational through action, tends naturally toward modes of being-together that we can justifiably call the mode of community. Being and community are inseparable."[46]

Thus, we have seen that for Clarke the human person, philosophically considered, is substantive, is active, is self-communicative, is relational, and is made for community. Clarke has begun to show this philosophically, building on the Aristotelian-Thomistic philosophical heritage.

Clarke continues to develop his ideas at some length. He sees that the innate drive of the human spirit toward the Good energizes human life.

> This innate, unrestricted drive of the human spirit ... toward the Infinite Good is the great hidden dynamo that energizes our whole lives, driving us on to ever new levels of growth and development, and refusing to let us be ultimately contented with any merely finite, especially material, good.[47]

For Clarke, the human person is on a historical journey toward a goal beyond this world. On this journey, the person creates him or herself through human actions. One also comes to knowledge through action:

---

[45] *Person and Being*, 13-14.

[46] *Person and Being*, 23.

[47] *Person and Being*, 37. See Deal W. Hudson, *Happiness and the Limits of Satisfaction* (Lanham, MD: Rowman & Littlefield, 1996).

One might well say that action and its implications is the primary key to the whole epistemology of Aquinas. All knowledge of the real for him is an interpretation of action. I know my own self because and insofar as I act. I know other things because, and insofar as, they act on me, and with all the implications thereof.[48]

For Clarke, one's coming to explicit self-awareness of being an "I" comes only through interaction with others. A person reaching out to us in love and treating us as a person enables us to come to a personal, though never complete, awareness and self-knowledge.[49] "The initial relationality of the human person towards the outer world of nature and other persons is primarily receptive, in need of actualizing its latent potentialities from without."[50] This process, of course, takes place over a lifetime. This human journey, I would think, might pass through various stages, as Francis de Sales notes in his *Introduction to the Devout Life* and his *Treatise on the Love of God*.[51]

This receptivity, Clarke mentions, is active, not merely passive. There is here really an interaction. Thus, Clarke adds a new insight here into the Salesian understanding of anthropology. Our "ecstatic personhood," if you will, both goes out to others and is receptive to others reaching out and interacting with us. We might compare this to "active listening" which is both receptive to the conversation of others but active in listening to the words and their implications with both head and heart. For Clarke, this receptivity differs from the receptivity in the Trinity in that the human person has potency in his or her receptivity while the divine persons are pure act.

---

[48] *Person and Being*, 90.

[49] See James Youniss, *Parents and Peers in Social Development* (Chicago: University of Chicago Press, 1980). Here he contends that children co-construct the world in relationship with one another. Youniss' studies would add empirical support to Clarke's philosophical argument.

[50] *Person and Being*, 72.

[51] St. Francis de Sales, *Introduction to the Devout Life*, Trans. with an Introduction and Notes, by John K. Ryan (Garden City, NY: Doubleday Image Books, 1966). I discuss stages of growth in St. Francis de Sales in my "Salesian Spirituality and Adult Developmental Psychology," chapter 3.

Human beings both give and receive. Human development in both giving and receiving occurs in communities, whose deepest roots are in loving communion. In such communities, persons are free to give wisdom and love. They are free to enter self-giving friendships. Such "authentic communities" liberate the self. To be is to be in communion with others and God. "We as finite persons acutely manifest ... both the ecstatic sharing, in imitation of our Source, because we are rich, and the ecstatic going out of ourselves in longing search for fulfillment, because we are poor."[52]

Ultimately, as one develops, he or she comes to "radically de-center" and focus more on God. This is the sort of transformation which normally occurs beyond mid-life or with certain extraordinary younger individuals, such as St. Terese of Lisieux. Clarke thus passes quite smoothly from his philosophical considerations of our humanness and self-transcendence in relationships and communities back to the theological aspects of our relationship with God.

In concluding this section, we might summarize by saying that Clarke stresses the dynamism of St. Thomas' "metaphysics of existential being." He proceeds by exploring:

> I. The Nature of Being, understood with the act of existence (*esse*) at its core, as dynamic, expansive act, first present in itself as "first act," then naturally pouring over in a "second act" to present itself to other in self-expression, self-communication, etc. through action.

Here he highlights the relational aspect of being. Then Clarke applies this to the person:

> II. Transfer to the Person. Since the person is not something added onto being from the outside, but the highest perfection and most intense expression of existential being itself, the person takes on more intensely the whole dynamism of existence as expansive, self-communicating act, now raised to the order of self-consciousness and freedom.[53]

---

[52] *Person and Being*, 101.

[53] *Person and Being*, 111.

Thus, we might say that the integrated person both knows self and can give self to others—precisely what we said on a theological basis in our earlier discussion of Salesian anthropology.

Friendship

With this philosophical grounding in the personalistic Thomism of Norris Clarke, we might turn to a few further considerations of the human person in St. Francis de Sales. In particular, we might comment briefly on friendship in De Sales' work. As we might expect, friendship is central in his thought and life.

Recent scholarly work shows the centrality of friendship to De Sales' life and spirituality. Elisabeth Stopp discusses St. Francis de Sales' view of friendship by drawing on his *Introduction to the Devout Life*, his *Treatise on the Love of God*, and his letters. Stopp discusses the virtue of love in DeSales' *Treatise*. She then notes the development of St. Francis' ideas on friendship as seen in the revised second edition of his *Introduction*:

> The relevant chapters in the definitive edition as compared with the *editio princeps* have been considerably revised and expanded .... St. Francis prepares the minds of his readers for a true understanding of friendship by first stressing the need for people to control their greed for instant gratification.[54]

After discussing these two major works, Stopp proceeds to elucidate two of St. Francis' closest friendships—those with his Italian Jesuit mentor, Antonio Possevino (1534-1611), and with "his fellow Savoyard, the lawyer Antoine Favre (1557-1624)."[55] She concludes that

> The relationship between Favre and St. Francis fulfilled what he had described in the *Introduction* as an ideal friendship in the world: two people going through life in a shared communication of all that is good and

---

[54] Elisabeth Stopp, "St. Francis de Sales: Attitudes to Friendship," in *A Man To Heal Differences: Essays and Talks on St. Francis de Sales* (Philadelphia: Saint Joseph's University Press, 1997), 125.

[55] Stopp, "St. Francis de Sales: Attitudes to Friendship," 127.

holy, giving one another courage and hope, urged on by the same spirit, working towards the same end in shared effort, shared affection."[56]

In a brief essay, Alexander Pocetto summarizes the Salesian teaching on friendship epitomized in De Sales' own friendships with Antoine Favre and St. Jane de Chantal (1572-1641). Among many significant points, he notes: that the union of spiritual friends does not destroy the individuality of the friends but heightens the development of their personal gifts; that "friends can differ in serious matters without destroying the friendship"; and that De Sales' friendships grew in that "He became very close friends of the spouses and children of his friends."[57]

James Langelaan considers "St. Francis' Philosophy of Friendship," in the course of his detailed investigation of the virtue of love as seen especially in De Sales' *Treatise*. Langelaan's "work in its broadest conception is a study of the philosophy and theology of love …."[58] He sees St. Francis' conception of friendship as his own blend of the thinking of Aristotle, Aquinas and Montaigne. In particular, Langelaan argues, with some nuance, that St. Francis de Sales offers a view of marriage with a "contemporary ring." "According to St. Francis' principle 'when love does not find us equal, it makes us equal,' husband and wife, who by nature are very unlike each other, are on the basis of their marriage friends on equal footing."[59]

Finally, in reviewing this recent scholarly work on friendship in St. Francis,[60] we come to the book *The Sweet and Gentle Struggle: Francis de Sales on the Necessity of Spiritual Friendship* by Dr. Terence A.

---

[56] Stopp, "St. Francis de Sales: Attitudes to Friendship," 134.

[57] A. T. Pocetto, O.S.F.S., "Spiritual Friendship in Salesian Spirituality," 4-5; available on the Internet at http://www4.desales.edu/~salesian/friendship.html.

[58] *The Philosophy and Theology of Love*, i.

[59] *The Philosophy and Theology of Love*, 57. The quotation is from the *Treatise*, II:57-59.

[60] I have offered a contemporary Salesian view of friendship in my *Friendship: The Key to Spiritual Growth* cited above.

McGoldrick.[61] In this thorough volume of almost 500 pages, McGoldrick traces the sources of the Salesian teaching in Aristotle, Augustine, Aelred, and Aquinas. He then discusses friendships in St. Francis' own life at some length. He concludes with a detailed exposition of the Salesian view of friendship. Though he modestly says that since Francis' thought defies easy categorization, others need not accept his interpretation, McGoldrick's work stands as the most thorough study of de Sales' views on friendship and the definitive one for our time.

For St. Francis de Sales, friendship is spiritual friendship. God, who made our hearts for loving, brings people together and provides us with friends as an aid to salvation.

> Friendship is therefore an integral part of Christian life. We see this in his own life by how completely he was willing to give himself to others, and yet never losing himself, because it was all balanced and integrated in a love of God and of himself. This ... is a difference with the classics. Whereas for them friendship was noble men sharing virtue in kindness and like ideals, for him it was always something oriented outside itself and of the persons, to Christ and in his bosom. Redemption gave his friendships a humble sacredness that was more understanding, more forgiving and yet more unyielding. It brought friendship into the intimacy of the Trinity and made its beginning, its development and its daily life something sacred.[62]

These expositions and reflections on Salesian friendship by four leading scholars indicate the centrality of relationships in De Sales' thinking. His personal life and his spiritual writing reflect this essential element of our humanity.

Concluding Reflections

In this modest essay, we have explored some important aspects of Salesian thought on the human person and reviewed some of the contemporary literature on Salesian Anthropology. In this context, we have sought to offer a further elaboration of Salesian thought.

---

[61] Lanham, MD: University Press of America, 1996. This was originally the author's doctoral thesis.

[62] *The Sweet and Gentle Struggle*, 496.

We have expanded our reflections on the Trinity to incorporate the contemporary notions of mutuality and receptivity. This implies that the human person, made in God's image, is oriented toward mutual and receptive relations with others.

We have proposed a link to personalistic Thomistic metaphysics to ground our Salesian work in realistic interpersonal philosophy. Thus, we contend that the person is both substantial and relational.

We have established the centrality of relationships in St. Francis own life and thought by reference to contemporary scholarly research. Thus, we have founded clearly our pastoral concern for spiritual relationships, small communities and local churches, while we have implicitly set the stage for future developments in our thinking about community.

We have alluded to the fact that individuals, relationships and communities develop or decline over time. It seems clear that the Salesian emphasis on spiritual progress or growth in virtue could be developed further in dialogue with the findings of our contemporary age.

We have raised the possibility that Salesian spirituality can also develop in relation to contemporary thinking on the acting person. We might also suggest that the precise nature and impact of such human action and interaction on moral and spiritual growth might be another arena for fruitful inquiry.

This essay reflects the challenge that our age presents to the Salesian spiritual tradition: to renew itself in dialogue with today's thought and experience. The present essay hopes to be a small step in that direction.

Chapter Four

The Christian Moral Life and Evangelization:

Contemporary Culture, Conscience, and the Magisterium

Dr. WILLIAM E. MAY

God loves us so deeply that he sent us his only-begotten Son to redeem us from sin and death and to make it possible for us to share forever his own divine life. This is the "good news," the Gospel, of Jesus. To make this good news known, loved, and efficacious is precisely what is meant by *evangelization,* which essentially consists in "bringing the Good News into every strata of humanity, and through its influence transforming humanity from within and making it new."[1]

Every Christian has a personal vocation and an indispensable role to play in the work of evangelization: to spread the Word of God, to make known the Good News of our salvation, in the world -- the cultural milieu -- in which he or she lives.

Here I hope to shed some light on the personal role that each Christian has to play in the work of evangelization. I will begin by considering the relationship between our lives as moral beings and culture, reflecting particularly on the character of contemporary culture and its understanding of human existence. I will then reflect on the understanding of

---

[1] Pope Paul VI, *Evangelii nuntiandi,* n. 18.

human existence and our vocation as taught by the Magisterium, and conclude with observations regarding the relationship between Magisterial teaching, the Catholic conscience, and the work of evangelization.

Culture and the Moral Life

Our moral life can, I believe, be described as an endeavor, cognitively, to come to know who we are and what we are to do if we are to be fully the beings we are meant to be, and, conatively, to do what we come to know we are to do if we are to be fully the beings we are meant to be. My attention here will focus on the *cognitive* aspect of this endeavor and the effect, for weal or woe, that culture has upon this struggle.

When we come into existence, when we are born, and when we are little children we do *not* yet know who we are or what we are to do if we are to be fully the beings we are meant to be. But we are divinely equipped to find out, because we are gifted with intelligence. But in order for us to exercise our intelligence it must first be developed, and in its development we can be both crippled or disabled and helped or enabled. As Christians we believe that Jesus, God's only-begotten Son-made-man and our Redeemer, is our "best and wisest friend,"[2] and that he has given us his Church to guide us and to enlighten our minds with the truth. The Church gives us immeasurable help in coming to know and appreciate who we are and what we are to do if we are to be fully the beings we are meant to be. But the culture in which we live can cripple and disable us or help and enable us in this cognitive endeavor.

As newborns we enter into the human world through a particular family, in a particular city or town and country, into a particular culture or set of cultures. The "world" we enter, as the theologian Bernard Lonergan, S.J., notes, is a world "mediated to us by meaning."[3] If these meanings are *true*, they enable and help us in our cognitive endeavor to come to know who we are and what we are to do if we are to be the beings we are meant to be; but if they are *false*, they can cripple us terribly in this endeavor.

---

[2] St. Thomas Aquinas, *Summa theologiae*, 1-2, q. 108, a.4, sed contra: "Christus est maxime sapiens et amicus."

[3] Bernard Lonergan, S.J., *Method in Theology* (New York: Herder & Herder, 1972), pp. 11-12.

These meanings are mediated to us, first of all, by the families into which we are born, and in particular by our mothers and fathers. And how blessed we are if we have good mothers and fathers who through their lives and example show us that in truth human life is sacred because it is the life of persons made in the image and likeness of God and called, in and through union with Jesus, to be his loving children. How blessed we are if our mothers and fathers love each other deeply and are faithful to their marital commitment, if they give themselves generously to their children and do all they can to help them realize their dignity as God's children and their obligations of love to their fellow men. But how tragic it is if one is born to a woman who does not even know who among her boyfriends may have fathered her child, or if one is abused as a baby, treated as a nuisance and pest, left to survive as best one can on one's own, or spoiled rotten. It is obvious that the "meanings" mediated in homes where God's love reigns, and those mediated in homes where it does not and where neither God nor his vicarious image, Man, is respected are quite different: the one set of meanings is enabling and helping; the other disabling and crippling.

But families are situated in a larger society, and the "meanings" meditated by this larger society have a powerful effect upon our endeavor to come to know who we are and what we are to do if we are to be fully the beings we are meant to be. The meanings the larger society mediate to us are constituted, in large measure, by the "culture" of that society. And that culture, in turn, is shaped by the actions and practices of the individuals who go to make it up. For the actions and practices of individuals, perhaps first only tolerated, will, if accepted and endorsed by the larger society, soon become embedded in that society's "way of life," in its customs and mores, in its laws and institutions, in short, in its "culture," its way of understanding what it means to be a human being. And there is evidently a great difference between a society shaped either greatly or even residually by a Christian understanding of human existence and one shaped by other understandings, including the secularist understanding dominant in contemporary Western societies.

Contemporary Western Secularistic Culture

Pope John Paul II devotes considerable attention in the first chapter of his encyclical *Evangelium vitae* to the characteristics of what he calls the "culture of death," which is an attitude or, better, an understanding of human existence more deeply rooted than public support for contraception, abortion, and euthanasia.[4]

According to his perceptive analysis, the culture of death is rooted in an understanding of the person that *"carries the concept of subjectivity to an extreme,"* recognizing "as a subject of rights only the person who enjoys full or at least incipient autonomy and who emerges from a state of total dependence on others" (n. 19). It asserts, furthermore, that human personal dignity rests upon *"the capacity for verbal and explicit,* or at least perceptible, *communication"* (n. 19). In short, on this view not all living human beings, not all members of the human species are persons, but only those able to care for themselves, to exercise autonomy, and to communicate to other conscious subjects: unborn babies, newborns, the severely brain damaged, the incompetent, simply do not count as persons. This understanding of human personhood is grounded, John Paul II says, "in a *notion of freedom* which exalts the isolated individual in an absolute way, and gives no place to solidarity, to openness with others and service of them" (n. 19).

The culture of death, precisely because it has lost the sense of God, leads to a loss of the sense of man himself, his personal dignity and the sanctity of human life. The culture of death does not regard man as "'mysteriously different' from other creatures"; he is considered, rather, "merely as one more living being, as an organism which, at most, has reached a very high stage of perfection." Man is "somehow reduced to being 'a thing'" (n. 22). As a result of this the human body "is no longer perceived as a properly personal reality, a sign and place of relations with others, with God, and with the world. It is reduced to pure materiality ... a complex of organs, functions and energies to be used according to the sole criteria of pleasure and efficiency" (n. 23). With the denigration of the body comes the depersonalization and trivialization of sex: "from being the sign, place and language of love, that is, of the gift of self and acceptance of another ... it increasingly becomes the occasion and instrument for self-assertion and the selfish satisfaction of personal desires and instincts" (n. 23).

---

[4] A very insightful study of Pope John Paul II's analysis of the "culture of death" is provided by Peter Casarella, "Evangelization and the Culture of Death," in *The Church's Mission of Evangelization: Essays in Honor of His Excellency the Most Reverend Agostino Cacciavillan,* ed. William E. May (Steubenville, OH: Franciscan University, 1996), pp. 103-128.

The culture of death also distorts the meaning of human suffering, failing "to perceive any meaning or value in suffering, but rather consider[ing] suffering the epitome of evil, to be eliminated at all costs" (n. 15).

In summary, I think it accurate to say that the secularist culture in which we live and which has given rise to the culture of death has the following characteristics: (1) it equates personhood with autonomy, independence, and the ability to communicate, and denies solidarity with the weak, the dependent, and the inarticulate, individuals who are, in effect, regarded as nonpersons; (2) it conceives man, male and female, merely as a highly evolved animal, in no way radically different in kind from other creatures; (3) it reduces the body, including sexuality, to a set of biological functions to be used by the person or conscious subject as he or she sees fit; and (4) it regards suffering as the epitome of evil, with no human meaning or significance. It is evident that the anthropology central to this culture is a dualism, sharply distinguishing between the personal, conscious, autonomous subject of experiences and the body that this subject uses, now for this purpose, now for that. Its morality is utilitarian and consequentialist; in this view, the moral task is to minimize suffering and maximize pleasure by the most technically efficient means possible.

This understanding of human existence is, I submit, a terribly crippling or disabling factor in our struggle, cognitively, to come to know who we are and what we are to do if we are to be fully the beings we are meant to be. Yet it is to men and women whose own self-understanding has been shaped by this culture -- to some extent at least, particularly if they are of the younger generation -- that the Good News of Jesus must be proclaimed today.

Human Existence and the Magisterium

First I will briefly summarize the Catholic understanding of Magisterium and then provide in some detail the understanding of human existence mediated to us through the Magisterium.

The Magisterium

Catholics believe that the Church is the "pillar of truth" (cf. 1 Tim 3.15). Jesus promised his apostles that he would not leave them orphans but would send his Holy Spirit to assist them (cf. Jn 14.16-17, 26; 15.26-27; 16.7-15; 20.21-22; Lk 24.49; Acts 1.8; 2.1-4). Within the Church the apostles held first place (cf. 1 Cor 12.28), for upon them the Church is established, both now and forever (cf. Eph 2.20; Rev 18,20). The apostles were chosen to receive God's revelation in Jesus; this revelation was not meant for them alone but for all humankind, to whom Jesus sent them to teach the truth (cf. Matt 28.20). The apostolic preaching, through which the revelation given by our Lord was communicated -- and successfully so -- to the apostolic Church, was, as Vatican Council II affirmed,

> to be preserved in a continuous line of succession until the end of time. Hence, the apostles, in handing on what they themselves had received, warn the faithful to maintain the traditions which they had learned either by word of mouth or by letter (cf. 2 Thess 2.15); and they warn the faithful to fight hard for the faith that had been handed over to them once and for all (cf. Jude 3). *What was handed on by the apostles comprises everything that serves to make the People of God live their lives in holiness and increase their faith.* In this way the Church, in her doctrine, life, and worship, perpetuates and transmits to every generation all that she herself is, all that she believes.[5]

Moreover, within the apostolic college Peter, the "rock" upon whom Jesus founded the Church (cf. Matt 16.16) and the one to whom Jesus had given the charge to confirm his brothers (Jn 21.15-17), was primary; he was the head of the apostolic college. Catholic faith holds that the authority given by Christ to Peter and the other apostles to teach in his name still exists in the Church. It is vested in the college of bishops, who are the successors to the apostles; and just as headship within the apostolic college was divinely given to Peter, so too in the college of bishops this headship is, by God's will, given to Peter's successor, the bishop of Rome. Thus, Vatican Council II clearly teaches:

> The divine mission, which was committed by Christ to the apostles, is destined to last until the end of the world (cf. Matt 28.20) .... Moreover, just as the office which the Lord confided to Peter alone, as first of the apostles, destined to be transmitted to his successors, is a permanent one,

---

[5] Vatican Council II, Dogmatic Constitution on Divine Revelation *(Dei Verbum)*, n. 8.

so also endures the office, which the apostles received, of shepherding the Church, a charge destined to be exercised without interruption by the sacred order of bishops. This sacred synod consequently teaches that the bishops have by divine institution taken the place of the apostles as pastors of the Church, in such wise that whoever listens to them is listening to Christ and whoever despises them despises Christ and him who sent Christ (cf. Lk 10.16).[6]

In short, "the task of authentically interpreting the word of God, whether written or handed on, has been entrusted exclusively to the teaching office of the Church, whose authority is exercised in the name of Christ."[7] This teaching office is vested in the Pope and the college of bishops under his headship. Catholic faith holds that this body has a more-than-human authority; it has the authority of Christ himself to make known to all human beings the saving truths of faith, including the saving truth about man, "the only creature on earth that God has wanted for its own sake,"[8] and whose full meaning, whose "mystery" becomes clear "only in the mystery of the Word made flesh."[9]

Magisterial Teaching and the Meaning of Human Existence

Since I cannot take up in detail all the rich understanding that the Magisterium mediates to us on this subject, my attention will focus on its teaching of the meaning of our existence as moral beings. I will do so by considering (1) the existential, religious significance of our everyday lives; (2) baptism as the fundamental choice or commitment of the Christian; and (3) the transformation of our entire existence by the love of God poured into our hearts at baptism.

---

[6] Vatican Council II, Dogmatic Constitution on the Church *(Lumen gentium)*, n. 20.

[7] *Dei Verbum*, n. 10.

[8] Vatican Council II, Pastoral Constitution on the Church in the Modern World *(Gaudium et spes)*, n. 24.

[9] *Gaudium et spes*, n. 22.

(1) The Existential, Religious Significance of Our Everyday Lives

Our everyday life is made up of what we "do" everyday. And what we "do," as the Magisterium teaches us, has existential, religious significance. This is beautifully shown by Pope John Paul II in his Encyclical *Veritatis splendor,* which he begins by meditating on the dialogue between Jesus and the rich young man who asked, "Teacher, what good must I do to have eternal life?" (Matt 19.16). Reflecting on this question, John Paul II says: "For the young man the question is not so much about rules to be followed, but *about the meaning of life* .... This question is ultimately an appeal to the absolute Good which attracts us and beckons us; it is the echo of a call from God who is the origin and goal of man's life" (n. 7). "It is," he continues, "*an essential and unavoidable question for the life of every man,* for it is about the moral good which must be done, and about eternal life" (n. 8).

The rich young man's question has religious and existential significance precisely because, as John Paul II emphasizes, it is in and through the actions we freely choose *to do* that we *determine ourselves* and give to ourselves our identity as persons. As the Pope says, "It is precisely through his acts that man attains perfection as man, as one who is called to seek his Creator of his own accord and freely to arrive at full and blessed perfection by cleaving to him" (n. 71). Our freely chosen deeds, he continues, "do not produce a change merely in the state of affairs outside of man but, to the extent that they are deliberate choices, they give moral definition to the very person who performs them, determining *his profound spiritual traits"* (n. 71). In developing this great truth the Holy Father calls to our attention a beautiful passage from St. Gregory of Nyssa's *De vita Moysis* (II, 2-3) that vividly expresses the existential, religious meaning of our daily deeds:

> All things subject to change and to becoming never remain constant, but continually pass from one state to another, for better or worse .... Now, human life is always subject to change; it needs to be born ever anew ... but here birth does not come about by a foreign intervention, as is the case with bodily beings ...; it is the result of a free choice. Thus we *are* in a certain sense our own parents, creating ourselves as we will, by our decisions (cited in n. 71).

Thus each free choice a person makes to *do* something (and this includes the free choice to *omit* doing something) involves "a *decision about oneself* and a setting of one's life for or against the Good, for or against the Truth, and ultimately for or against God" (n. 65). We can consequently conclude that our *character,* or "the integral, existential identity of the person -- the entire person in all his or her dimensions,"[10] is shaped by the choices, good and bad, that we make every day of our lives.

In other words, we make ourselves *to be* the persons we are in and through the free, self-determining choices we make every day of our lives. If the choices we make are *good*, that is, in accordance with the truth -- whose ultimate source is God himself -- we will make ourselves (with his help) fully to be the beings we are meant to be, the beings God wills us to be.

(2) Baptism as the Fundamental Choice or Option of the Christian

Every free choice is self-determining and hence has existential and religious significance. But, as John Paul II points out, it is correct to emphasize "the importance of certain choices which shape a person's entire moral life, and which serve as bounds within which other particular everyday choices can be situated and allowed to develop" (n. 65). The Pope recognizes, in short, the critical significance of certain kinds of choices that can correctly be called "commitments."

An excellent example of a choice of this kind, a fundamental commitment, is the choice to marry. Marriage comes into being only when a man and a woman, forswearing all others, "give" themselves to one another as husband and wife through an act of "irrevocable personal consent."[11] Through this act of free choice they give themselves a new identity -- the identity of husband and wife, of spouses -- and they commit themselves to respect and foster throughout their life together the "blessings" or "goods" of marriage: faithful, spousal love and the having and raising of children. They are henceforth obliged, by virtue of their

---

[10] On this see Germain Grisez, *The Way of the Lord Jesus*, Vol. 1, *Christian Moral Principles* (Chicago: Franciscan Herald Press, 1983), p. 59.

[11] *Gaudium et spes,* n. 48.

marital commitment, to integrate the other things they choose to do in such a way that they can harmonize with this fundamental choice or commitment. The choice to get married is truly a choice that "shapes" a person's entire moral life and it serves as "bounds within which other particular everyday choices can be situated and allowed to develop."

An even more fundamental or basic commitment or choice of the Christian -- indeed, his or her most fundamental commitment -- is the free choice, made only with the help of God's saving grace, *to be* a Christian. Pope John Paul II underscores this great truth, emphasizing that the "choice of Freedom" which "Christian moral teaching, even in its Biblical roots, acknowledges [as fundamental]...is the decision of faith, of the *obedience of faith* (cf. Rom 16.26)." This is the free choice, he then continues, "by which man makes a total and free self-commitment to God, offering "the full submission of intellect and will to God as he reveals" (n. 66).[12]

This fundamental choice or commitment of the Christian is, of course, his or her *baptismal commitment* or choice *to be* a Christian, a living member of Christ's body, the Church.[13] One enters into communion with Jesus, becoming one of his people, the Church, in and through baptism. And at the heart of baptism is a free, self-determining choice, one made possible by God's saving grace, and this choice commits the Christian to live henceforward *as a Christian,* i.e., as truly a child of God and brother or sister of Jesus, whose only will, like that of Jesus himself, is to do what is pleasing to the Father. This means that the Christian freely commits himself or herself to integrate *all* his or her choices, *all* the things that he or she does every day, into this basic commitment. Because he or she has "put on" Christ, the Christian is called *to be* Christ's "vicar" in the world in which he or she lives.

Most of us were baptized as infants who, at the time, could not make free choices of our own. But others, our godparents, stood as our proxies, responding in our name to the call to die to sin and live in a way worthy

---

[12] This passage from *Veritatis splendor* is a citation from Vatican Council II, Dogmatic Constitution on the Church *(Lumen gentium),* n. 5, which in turn quotes a passage from Vatican Council I, Dogmatic Constitution on the Catholic Faith *(Dei Filius),* ch. 3, DS 3008.

[13] Grisez develops this idea marvelously in *Christian Moral Principles*, pp. 551 ff.

of God's own children. As we grew in the household of the faith, we renewed our baptismal commitment when we received the sacrament of confirmation; and we are given the chance to renew this fundamental commitment of our lives frequently, particularly during the Easter Vigil.

In and through this fundamental choice or option, the Christian freely takes upon himself or herself the task and honor of sharing in Christ's redemptive work. The Christian's sublime mission is to complete, in his or her own flesh, "what is lacking in Christ's afflictions for the sake of his body, the Church" (Col 1.24). We Christians, in short, are "to be what we are!"[14] -- living vicars of Jesus himself, imaging him in our own daily lives, cooperating with him in redeeming others and, indeed, in redeeming the entire cosmos.

Precisely because of baptism Christians are called to *holiness,* to sanctity: "All in the Church," the Fathers of Vatican Council II insist, "whether they belong to the hierarchy or are cared for by it, are called to holiness, according to the apostle's saying -- For this is God's will, your sanctification (1 Thess 4.3; cf. Eph 1.4). This holiness...is expressed in many ways by individual Christians who, each in his own state of life, tend to the perfection of love."[15] "It is therefore quite clear," the Council Fathers continue, "that *all Christians in any state of or walk of life are called to the fullness of Christian life and to the perfection of love.*"[16]

But how can this be, and what does this mean for our existence as moral beings?

(3) Christian Love and the Transformation of Our Lives as Moral Beings

By choosing to be baptized and to make themselves, with God's help, *to be* Christians, human persons commit themselves to a life of perfection, of holiness. But what does this mean, and how is it even possible?

---

[14] On this great Pauline theme see George P. Montague, S.M., *Maturing in Christ* (Milwaukee: Bruce, 1964), pp. 92-100; see also Manuel Miguens, O.F.M., "On Being a Christian: Pauline Perspectives," in *Principles of Catholic Moral Life,* ed. William E. May (Chicago: Franciscan Herald Press, 1981), pp. 89-110.

[15] *Lumen gentium,* n. 39.

[16] *Lumen gentium,* n. 40.

It is possible because God, who enables us to accept baptism in living faith, gives to us through baptism *his very own life*. Now, as Christians, we are really "new creatures" in Christ; we share in his divine nature just as truly as he shares in our human nature. In and through the grace and love of God poured into our hearts at baptism we are literally divinized: we become truly members of the divine family, brothers and sisters of Jesus and able, with him, to call his Father "our" Father, inwardly led by his Spirit.

As new beings in Christ we are called to an end that utterly surpasses human understanding -- eternal life with God himself -- and this life begins, the Magisterium teaches us, *here and now*. To enable us, his children, to attain this end and to live here and now worthily as his very own sons and daughters, God gives us a "law" that brings to fulfillment and perfection the "natural law" written in our hearts. This new law, communicated in its fullness to human persons by Jesus through the gift of his Spirit, is the "gospel law," the "law of new and everlasting covenant," the "law of love." And, as St. Thomas teaches, what is "most powerful in the law of the new covenant, and in which its whole power consists, is the grace of the Holy Spirit, which is given to Christ's faithful."[17] This law, unlike the natural law written in our hearts or the Mosaic law written on the tablets of stone, not only gives us the knowledge of what we are to do if we are to be fully the beings we are meant to be, it also inwardly enables us, St. Thomas says, *to do* everything necessary to live as God wills us to.[18] Although we are still capable of sinning after our regeneration in the waters of baptism, the new law given to us in Jesus, "insofar as it is considered in itself, gives us sufficient help that we can avoid sin."[19] This law is the law of Christ's self-giving love,[20] a love that *enables* us to live worthily as his brothers and sisters, as persons commissioned to share personally in his redemptive work.

---

[17] St. Thomas Aquinas, *Summa theologiae*, 1-2, q. 106, a. 1.

[18] *Summa theologiae*, 106, 1, ad 2.

[19] *Summa theologiae*, 106, 2, ad 2.

[20] *Summa theologiae*, 107, 1, ad 2.

Jesus gives us, his co-redeemers, a new commandment: we are to love even as we have been and are loved by God in Jesus, that is, with a redemptive, saving kind of love. As Jesus said, "A new commandment I give to you: love one another even as I have loved you" (Jn 13.34), and he went on to say, "As the Father has loved me, so have I loved you: abide in my love" (Jn 15.9). If we "abide" in Jesus' love, he and his Father and Spirit will "abide" in us, empower us to live truly as Christ's vicars. Jesus' own self-giving love, therefore, is the *existential principle of the Christian life*.[21] It is its existential principle precisely because it makes Christian life, a life of holiness and of self-giving love, possible.

This is clearly the teaching of the Magisterium. Jesus, as John Paul II insists in *Veritatis splendor,* reveals to us that authentic human "freedom is acquired in *love,* that is, in the *gift of self*...the gift of self *in service to God and one's brethren"* (n. 87). He further points out that "those who live 'by the flesh' experience God's law as a burden," while those "who are impelled by love and 'walk in the Spirit' (Gal 5.16) ... find in God's law the fundamental and necessary way in which to practice love as something freely chosen and freely lived out" (n. 18). Men and women *can,* with God's never-failing grace, "abide" in love (cf. n. 24).

We know, and the Magisterium constantly reminds us, that mortal sin is utterly incompatible with the Christian life. A person sins mortally whenever he "knowingly and willingly, for whatever reason, chooses something gravely disordered" (n. 70), and we can be sure that were are sinning mortally if we choose to do any kind of deed which the Church, through her Magisterium, identifies as utterly incompatible with God's holy law because it gravely violates the good of the person made in his image (cf. nn. 78-80).

But if we are to be holy as God, our Father is holy, we must do far more than avoid mortal sin. We must root out venial sin as well. I fear that most of us have our own favorite venial sins, little sins that we enjoy and simply do not want to give up because we *like* to do them: for instance, taking delight over the discomfitures experienced by people we do not like, gossiping, telling "little" lies to avoid the unpleasant consequences we would have to face were we to be truthful, etc. In short, most of us are not saints even though we know that we are called to sanctity. We are still very imperfect children of God, unwilling,

---

[21] On divine love as the existential principle of the Christian life see Grisez, *Christian Moral Principles,* pp. 599-623.

unfortunately, to follow Jesus as we should, to take up our own cross daily and thus carry out his work of redemption.

The great doctors of the Church and the Magisterium, however, remind us of our vocation to holiness. They urge us to study the Scriptures and to realize that the Lord's Sermon on the Mount (Matt 5) gives us, as St. Augustine said many centuries ago, "The *perfect pattern of the Christian life.*"[22] Indeed, as St. Thomas says, the Lord's Sermon on the Mount "contains completely the information needed for the Christian life. In it the inner movements of the person are perfectly ordered."[23]

The Magisterium, too, seeks to open our minds and hearts to the meaning of the Lord's Sermon on the Mount and to the deep significance of the Beatitudes for understanding just what the Christian moral life entails and precisely what the requirements of Christian love are.[24] In particular, Pope John Paul II tries to do this in *Veritatis splendor*. With Augustine he calls the Lord's Sermon on the Mount the *"magna charta* of Christian morality" (n. 15). In this Sermon Jesus had emphasized that he had come not "to abolish the Law and the Prophets" but "to fulfill them" (Matt 5.17). John Paul II says that *"Jesus brings the commandments to fulfillment ... by interiorizing their demands and by bringing out their fullest meaning"* (n. 15). The Beatitudes of the Sermon on the Mount, he continues, "speak of the basic attitudes and dispositions in life and therefore they *do not coincide exactly with the commandments.* "On the other hand," he says, "*there is no separation or opposition* between the Beatitudes and the commandments: both refer to the good, to eternal life" (n. 16). They are, John Paul II writes, "above all *promises*, from which there also indirectly flow *normative indications* for the moral life .... [T]hey are a sort of *self-portrait of Christ...invitations to discipleship and to communion of life with Christ"* (n. 16).

---

[22] St. Augustine, *The Lord's Sermon on the Mount*, I, 1; trans. John J. Jepson, S.S., in *Ancient Christian Writers*, No. 5 (Westminster, MD: Newman, 1948), p. 11.

[23] *Summa theologiae*, 1-2, 108, 3.

[24] In his *Credo of the People of God,* n. 12, Pope Paul VI stressed that the Beatitudes of the Sermon on the Mount can be regarded as the model summary of the uniquely Christian content of Jesus' moral teaching.

This passage from *Veritatis splendor* is pregnant with meaning. The Christian moral life is, first and foremost, a following of Christ. But we follow him, John Paul II instructs us, not by any outward imitation but by *"becoming conformed to him* who became a servant even to giving himself up on the Cross (cf. Phil 2.58)" (n. 21). Following Christ means *"holding fast to the very person of Christ"* (n. 19). Precisely because the Beatitudes are, as the Pope says, "a sort of *self-portrait of Christ"* (n. 16), it follows that by shaping our choices and actions in accord with the Beatitudes we will ever more deeply act in accord with Jesus' new command of love and progress toward the holiness to which we are called.

I believe that among contemporary theologians Germain Grisez has articulated most clearly the role that the Beatitudes are meant to play in Christian existence and how they enable Christian men and women truly to "portray" Christ in their lives. They are, as Grisez says, "modes of Christian response," ways of responding to the challenges of everyday life with true Christian love. They are internal dispositions, inclining the Christian to do only what is pleasing to the Father. They are Christian virtues, and, as rooted in God's gift of divine love, they can be rightly regarded as "gifts" of his spirit. If we look upon the Beatitudes in this way, the requirements of Christian love, Grisez suggests, can be expressed as follows:

1. *To expect and accept all good, including the good fruits of one's work, as God's gift* -- for the "poor in spirit" understand that their achievements are only a share, given freely and generously by God, in his fullness. The virtuous disposition is humility; the Christian vice is pride. The corresponding gift of the Holy Spirit is fear of the Lord.

2. *To accept one's limited role in the Body of Christ and fulfill it* -- for the "meek" understand that submissiveness to God's will involves no loss or delay to their personal fulfillment. The virtuous disposition is "Christian dedication," while lukewarmness and minimalism are opposed to it. The corresponding gift of the Spirit is piety or godliness, an attitude of filial reverence and dutifulness toward God.

3. *To put aside or avoid everything which is not necessary or useful in the fulfillment of one's personal vocation* -- for those who "mourn" (not only contrite sinners but all those who turn from transient goods to fulfillment in Jesus) understand that to be disposed to goodness itself frees one from the pursuit of particular, finite goods for their own sake. The virtuous disposition is detachment; worldliness and anxiety are opposed

dispositions. The corresponding gift of the Spirit is knowledge, by which one discerns what belongs to faith and judges everything by its light.

4. *To endure fearlessly whatever is necessary or useful for the fulfillment of one's personal vocation* -- for those who "hunger and thirst for righteousness" understand that they have nothing whatsoever to fear. The virtuous disposition is the faithfulness and heroism characteristic of the martyr, although required of all Christians, while weakness of faith and faintheartedness in the face of non-Christian standards are among the Christian vices. The corresponding gift of the Spirit is fortitude.

5. *To be merciful according to the universal and perfect measure of mercy which God has revealed in Jesus* -- for those who "are merciful" understand that they are to be disinterested and selfless as God is. The virtuous disposition is mercy, compassion, service to others on the model of Jesus, while the opposed vice is a legalistic attitude toward others. The gift of the Spirit is counsel.

6. *To strive to conform one's whole self to living faith, and purge anything which does not meet this standard* -- for the "pure of heart" understand that in this life charity requires continuous conversion. The virtuous disposition is single-minded devotion to God, including a sense of sin and continuing conversion, while the Christian vice is reflected in mediocrity and insincerity. The corresponding gift of the Spirit is understanding.

7. *To respond to evil with good, not with resistance, much less with destructive action* -- for the "peacemakers" understand that the effort to live according to divine love must be universally conciliatory. The virtuous disposition is the conciliatoriness which seeks the redemption of enemies; one opposed disposition is the tendency to shun evil instead of carrying on a redemptive ministry to those enslaved by it. The corresponding gift of the Spirit is wisdom, the power of putting in order as peacemakers do.

8. *To do no evil that good might come of it, but suffer evil together with Jesus in cooperation with God's redeeming love* -- for "those persecuted for righteousness' sake" understand that one must undergo evil in order to bring the evildoer in touch with perfect goodness. The virtuous disposition is self-oblation, the Christian vice the fragile rectitude of the person who does not wish to sin but seeks fulfillment in this world. Since there are only seven gifts, Augustine assigns none here; however, one might say that there is a corresponding gift, unique to each Christian, and disposing him or her to offer God the unique gift of himself or herself.[25]

---

[25] Grisez, *Christian Moral Principles*, pp. 654-655.

The Beatitudes, in other words, internally dispose us to be true vicars of Christ, portraying him in our lives. They specify ways of acting that mark a person whose will, enlivened by the love of God poured into his or her heart, seeks to live out the vocation of all Christians to holiness and to carry out, in particular, the uniquely indispensable role that God has given to him or her to carry on the redemptive work of his only-begotten Son, Jesus Christ.

In summary, according to the Magisterium, men and women differ radically in kind from other animals because, being made in the image and likeness of God, they are gifted with intelligence and awesome freedom to determine their own lives by the free choices they make every day. Moreover, as John Paul II reminds us in *Veritatis splendor*, "it is only in the mystery of the Word incarnate that light is shed on the mystery of man," because it is Christ, the last Adam, who fully discloses man to himself and unfolds his noble calling by revealing the mystery of the Father and the Father's love (n. 2).[26] In and through baptism men and women become united to Christ, sharing his divine nature just as he shares their human nature. Through the choice to be baptized, moreover, men and women commit themselves to the following of Christ, to share in his redemptive work, to be, like him, true children of his loving Father, willing and able, because of the love he pours into their hearts, to shape their lives and actions in accordance with the Beatitudes and in this way attain the holiness to which they are called and to *be* Christ to those whom they meet everyday of their lives.

Magisterium, Conscience, and Evangelization

Here I will be brief, for I do not want, nor is there need, to develop a treatise on conscience. Basically, conscience means our awareness of moral truth. Thus, it in no way encloses man within himself but rather opens him to God and to others. Conscience is *not* the source or origin of truth -- God is -- but, as Vatican Council II teaches us, it is through the mediation of conscience that we come to recognize ever increasingly the unchanging truth of God's wise and loving plan for human existence.[27]

---

[26] The internal reference in this passage is to *Gaudium et spes*, n. 22.

[27] See Vatican Council II, Declaration on Religious Liberty *(Dignitatis humanae)*, n. 3.

Conscience opens us up not only to God but to our fellow human beings, who can help us become more and more aware of the moral truth that we need in order to shape our lives rightly. Our consciences, in other words, must be formed or, better, *informed*. Unfortunately, they can also be *misinformed* by the false meanings about human existence mediated through various channels, and in particular today, by the "culture of death."

One who wants to find out the truth about something should seek it from a trustworthy source. Thus, if one were inquiring about one's health, one realizes that a doctor is a far more trustworthy source than a barber, no matter how competent the barber might be in his line of work or how friendly and sympathetic he is as a person. Catholics can be confident that in their search for moral truth, the truth that has its ultimate source in God's wise and loving plan for human existence, they can find it in the teaching of the Magisterium, for the Magisterium is Jesus' gift to them. In *Veritatis splendor* John Paul II puts the matter quite well when he says:

> Christians have a great help for the formation of conscience *in the Church and her Magisterium*. As the [Second Vatican] Council affirms: "In forming their consciences the Christian faithful must give careful attention to the sacred and certain teaching of the Church. For the Catholic Church is by the will of Christ the teacher of truth. Her charge is to announce and teach authentically that truth which is Christ, and at the same time with her authority to declare and confirm the principles of the moral order which derive from human nature itself."[28] It follows that the authority of the Church, when she pronounces on moral questions, in no way undermines the freedom of conscience of Christians. This is not only because freedom of conscience is never freedom "from" the truth but always and only freedom "in" the truth, but also because the Magisterium does not bring to the Christian conscience truths which are extraneous to it; rather it brings to light the truths which it ought already to possess, developing them from the starting point of the primordial act of faith (n. 64).

The Pope has put matters very well. The teaching of the Magisterium about the meaning of our existence as human, moral persons is simply to remind us, in the light of God's revelation, who we are and what we are to do if we are to be fully the beings we are meant to be, the beings God

---

[28] *Dignitatis humanae*, n. 14.

wants us to be. God has graciously revealed to us that we are not only his living icons or images, but his beloved children, now one with his only-begotten Son-made-man, Jesus Christ, and summoned to be saints and to bring to the world in which we live the redeeming and saving words of eternal life. We are to carry on Christ's redemptive work by evangelizing the society in which we live, building a "culture of life" and a "civilization of love" to take the place of the "culture of death" that unfortunately has become rooted in many places in the world today.

Christian laymen and laywomen are called to carry out the redemptive work of Christ, which inescapably entails evangelization, *in the secular world in which they live.*[29] Blessed Josemaria Escriva, the founder of Opus Dei, expressed this great truth regarding the specific call of the lay faithful to carry out their vocation to holiness *in the world* quite accurately by saying: "Everyday life is the true setting place for your lives as Christians. Your ordinary contact with God takes place where your fellow men, your yearnings, your work and your affections are. There you have your daily encounter with Christ. *It is in the midst of the most material things of the earth that we must sanctify ourselves, serving God and all mankind."*[30]

All Christians have the common vocation to holiness, which they achieve by cooperating with Jesus in his redemptive work. But each one of us has a personal vocation, for God wants each one of us to share in a uniquely personal and indispensable way, in this redemptive work. One of our most serious obligations, therefore, is to discover precisely what our personal vocation is and then to carry out faithfully, knowing that Jesus, "our best and wisest friend," will give us the grace needed to do so.

---

[29] See *Lumen gentium,* n. 11 on the secular character of the lay Catholic.

[30] Blessed Josemaria Escriva, "Passionately Loving the World," in *Conversations with Monsignor Escriva* (Manila: Sinag-Tala Publishers, 1985), n. 113.

Part II:

Topics in
Moral & Pastoral Theology

Chapter Five

Reviving the Sixth Commandment with Fr. John Harvey, O.S.F.S.

Rev. Msgr. GEORGE A. KELLY

The Sixth Commandment may still be alive in our American culture, but it surely is gasping for breath in the average urban household. Everyone, it seems, is doing sex nowadays. If not denying the possibility of chastity or the need of virginity, they are at least carrying condoms on a date, or cohabiting, or sexually abusing their own children, actions unthinkable a few generations ago. Far beyond these novelties in American family life are the foot-long needles piercing pregnant women and their fetuses who, flailing their little arms and legs, drown in potassium chloride. Seniors remember yesterdays when Catholic high school students were virgins, and when their parents remained married till death did them part, and how a member of the United States Senate was driven from political life for his dalliance with the wrong woman.

The sexual revolution has done its work, and the social results are not clean. Once upon a time "progressives," in and out of the Catholic community, complained that the Church was too preoccupied with sex. In view of the present state of America's sex life, was she? What sins would be prevalent, do you think, even in a reasonably Christian society? Blasphemy? Murder? Bank robbing? Hardly! The Sixth Commandment may not be God's first commandment, but historically its violation has brought more Catholics to confession than the others. Why not? Thomas Aquinas once warned how lust leads even to loss of faith.

When the sexual revolution made inroads into the Church, priests with laity arose to defend Catholic teaching. Early in the 1960s, Fr. John

Ford, S.J., with help from Germain and Jeannette Grisez, led the Catholic charge against Catholic capitulation to contraception. Msgr. John Christopher Knott, aided by married couples across the country, spearheaded the Church's defense of indissoluble marriage from the *Family Life Bureau* (Washington, DC). Cardinals like Terence J. Cooke and John J. O'Connor, along with "patriarchs" of the pro-life movement such as Drs. John R. Stanton and Herbert Ratner, became the Church's symbols of life to a "culture of death."

In 1980 Fr. John F. Harvey, O.S.F.S., came forth to become the Church's apostle to homosexuals and her voice to those who would persuade Catholics that homosexuality is good. His endeavor, aptly named *Courage,* takes its place on a long list of Catholic social apostolates which give witness to the faith in a world whose leaders are deaf to its good sense. Many such apostolates aim their sight on poverty, on workers' rights, on war, on totalitarianism, and on sins related thereto. Fr. Harvey's apostolate concerns the wholesome use of sexuality and its relation to the American family, on which the nation and the Church depend more than on any other single private institution.

The Church and the Lay Apostolates

Whenever an important social apostolate finds its way into the lifelines of the Church, a priest is often in the vanguard. Sometimes he is impelled there by lay activists, or sometimes he is inspired by something a pope wrote or an older priest urged. The better ones enter this world not as political ideologues, but as a voice of Christ, interested in alleviating distress or oppression, but awakening in them the love of God. From the days of the first deacons, the Church has always been interested in people's temporal well-being (Acts 6). People belong to her as well as the State, even if her special role is to make them conscious of their eternal destiny (Mt. 10:28). The State, for example, might cure *AIDS* without having a compelling interest in the moral habits of its victims, but the priest must devote his energies to both. More than seventy years ago Pius XI insisted that a Catholic social apostolate, if it would fitfully reconstruct a malfunctioning public institution, must give high priority to the reform of its morals. Replacing rascals with a new set of rascals is hardly an act of legitimate reform.

The priest reformers of the early 20th century were one with Pius XI in that conviction. Msgr. John A. Ryan, in its first decades, became "the father of Catholic social reconstruction." John La Farge, S.J., and Dom Virgil Michel, O.S.B., respectively sought racial justice and better Catholic worship in the 1920's. In the 1930's Msgr. John P. Monaghan helped establish the *Association of Catholic Trade Unionists*, while in the 1940's Msgr. Reynold Hillenbrand was a leading reformer in the *Christian Family Management* and kindred apostolates. (While Dorothy Day's *Catholic Worker Movement* was precious to many priests [e.g., Paul Hanly Furfey], this lay woman remained the most prominent personality in her field of endeavor.)

Driven by their "zeal for God" (Rom. 10:2), these priests of the Church were firm believers that their role in mundane affairs was subsidiary to that of the Catholic laity, because they were duty bound to outline the Catholic direction and to oversee the zealots' spiritual life. Although the Church has been speaking of the lay apostolate prior to both the French and Industrial revolutions, at least since Benedict XIV (1740-1758), yet her influence on what was left of Christian Europe had long since waned. Enlightenment visionaries, later industrial barons and government bureaucrats, championed pragmatic politics (i.e., the democratic process) as the ultimate determinator of the world's business. Cutting secular society from its Christian roots and isolating the voice of clerics from the mainstream of society, became their stock in trade, unless, of course, parsons and priests reinforced the secular vision of the world's kingdom and reinforced their hegemony over its structures. Without the lay voice, the Word of God would hardly be heard in the public square, or so the argument went.

Catholic political parties, labor unions, or governments eventually went the way of Christian Kings and Papal States. Experiments like "worker priests," whatever help they might have been to individual workers, proved to be no help to the Church. Indeed, Pius XII shifted gears somewhat, when in 1957 he downgraded Australia's powerful lay *Catholic Social Movement,* a political center dominated by laity and engaged in hard politics over many years with the approval of the hierarchy, into a catechetical organization under the bishops' total control. Melbourne's Archbishop Daniel Mannix submitted to the pope on that one, but remained unhappy with the Church's step backward. Many years later (1971), at the mention of Mannix's name, Paul VI, who was at that time Secretary to Pius XII, mused aloud: "Ah, yes, a different man for a different age. We no longer can do the things we could do then." The Roman hopes for a vigorous lay influence on a country's politics had dimmed, in part because of the timidity of leading bishops.

The Demoralization of Catholicity

Of course, Paul VI spoke about Mannix a half dozen years after Vatican II, when leaders of many Catholic apostolates no longer believed in principle that there was a single Catholic answer to personal or social difficulties, let alone one in practice. Biblical exegetes were saying that scripture gave little scientific basis to Christ's establishment of the Church. Dogmatic theologians, using historicism as a research tool, relativized many creedal propositions so that their realistic meaning might be interpreted to mean something other than what *The Catechism of the Catholic Church* says they are. Proportionalist moralists, denying the existence of absolute and unexceptional moral norms, made "let your conscience be your guide" a valid norm for Catholic decision-making.

Not only did these savants relativize the hierarchy's role in forming Christ-like consciences, but they provided aid and comfort to secularists, whose media gave them immediate approval. They were "progressives" for democratizing Catholic decision-making, even about faith and morals. Those alleged "scientific" theories about Catholicity, widely propagated in Catholic catechesis after Vatican II, helped dilute among the faithful the very notion of "divine revelation," and of Christ as "The Word of God." Gabriel Moran, once a prominent catechetical icon of American Catholic educators, openly declared in 1997 that the very notion of "revealed religion" is dead. Science killed it, he says. Faith in God, Christ, or Church is a man-made phenomenon, not God's gift to mankind. The secularists were happy with these developments because the more believing Catholics made peace with a culture fashioned by the mind of Voltaire and the Encyclopedists, of Karl Marx, of Sigmund Freud, or of Carl Rogers, the more the Church lost battles in the public square over the place of "revealed religion" in modern society, and the less necessity for "Ten Commandments" to be the foundations of American mores or law. Could the Church expect otherwise, if bishops were marginalized in the game of street politics and a Catholic lay apostolate was nonexistent?

The most obvious victims of the secular conquest of the American culture were the sacrament of Matrimony and the Sixth Commandment, both vital to the stability of family life. At the time of the country's founding, Protestant Divines might not have recognized marriage as a sacrament, but they surely believed that the Sixth Commandment remained the country's moral base. By the time of the Bicentennial only

Orthodox Jews, Evangelical Protestants, and Roman Catholics still defended the Decalogue as sound public policy and good guidance. All three groups are now looked upon by elites as retrogrades of a dying or dead era. "Thou shalt not have strange gods before me" and "Though shalt not commit adultery" were replaced by "born free," "think free," "choose free." "Sex for sex' sake" — like "art for art's sake" or "news for news' sake" — became the new "moral" maxims. A "right of privacy" was discovered in the Constitution, though the Founding Fathers forgot to place it there. Hitherto it was unapplied to most life situations, such as going to war or paying taxes. And even today it does not apply to compulsory seat belts and nonsmoking. In practice, the American government now professes to have no vested interest in sex *in actu,* although, as everyone knows, the cost of the *misuse of sex* to the fabric and character of the country transcends the billions of dollars expended on the social disorder that is its birth-child. Elites blame the country's fall from cultural grace worldwide on everything but the disintegration of the American family, not only the half-empty nest but the nest too often without father or mother present full-time.

It has been a truism of bible history that whenever "man" became his own "god" he created his own idols to worship, one of which is sex — readily available at little cost, if any, by instinct a lot of fun, and private. The God of Abraham may be merciful, but is frequently vengeful toward those who violate the family orientation, who use it wrongly, or abuse its natural aptitudes. Sexual choices made in opposition to God's providential guidance in the Ten Commandments, prompted the Psalmist, in his first song, to give warning: "Wicked ways lead to doom." How few sinners realize, until too late, how much human happiness in this life follows goodness, not wickedness.

Nonetheless, in secularized society, as always, there are no wicked ways, unless the State says so. The secularists propose this as a given. They replace God's prophets with their politicians, whose guiding principle is *bonum est utile.* Nothing itself is evil. If a thing is useful, it is good. This principle brings Pontius Pilate to mind, the politician who sent Christ to the Cross, though he knew him to be innocent. The crowd wanted Barabbas; it was as simple as that.

During the 1960's, as the sexual revolution in America unfolded, contraception became the national cure for all unhappiness and also an aid to upward mobility and psychological contentment. On the world scene it was the prudent response to the population problem and a proper prevention of war by countries looking for *lebensraum*. Its use, they said, also marked the end of "back alley" abortions.

Long before Paul VI, who was clear about the social evils inherent in contraceptionism, an Anglican bishop-theologian named Charles Gore stripped the contraceptive corpus down to its bare bones. Standing before his episcopal peers at a Lambeth Conference in 1930 he argued: If sexuality and its exercise by married couples is severed from childbearing, so that the companionship or pleasure components of a sexual relationship become values in themselves, unrelated to the family meaning of the marital union, then there was no reason on earth why the unmarried might not legitimately opt for the same companionship or pleasure without worrying about the necessity of marriage or about the misadventure of parenthood. No reason either, he added, why homosexuals and lesbians should be denied the value of sexual orgasm, even if they achieved this in other than the normal way.

Bishop Gore was right, of course, for anyone but utilitarians. Up until then, Christian contraceptionists hid their condoms in the back drawer of a drug store, whereas today they have high visibility at the cashier's drawer and are distributed freely to public school teenagers. Back in 1930, Pius XI went Gore one step further by labeling contraceptive use as "an offense against the law of God, and those who indulge in it are branded with the guilt of a grave sin." The holistic view of Christian marriage was so imbedded in Catholic culture at the time of *Casti Connubii*, that a generation later one Jesuit moralist in Rome looked upon contraceptive practices as sins against the Catholic faith, as they were against the sacrament of Matrimony.

This was standard Catholic thinking until the 1960s, when "the contraceptive mentality," not unlike "the slave mentality" of the Roman Empire, was institutionalized in the reigning culture of the West, no one exalting it as a saintly state of mind, but everyone overwhelmed by its presence and doing its business. There was some excuse for the Romans. They did not know the God of Abraham, Isaac and Jacob. And they crucified Jesus.

The outer limits of the *bonum est utile* principle in action, at least for society, is reached when prominent thinkers, in control of its power structures, teach that sexual relations between persons of the same sex are good, or can be normal, or at least are viable options for those who choose that relationship. The homosexual lobby has achieved its success in gaining a certain measure of popular acceptance precisely on that basis.

The Church's political response to all these modern challenges, from contraception to sodomy, has been timid, primarily because so many in-house Catholic dissenters accept relativist morality. If their kind, working in the secular environment, did to *The New York Times* or to the *American Civil Liberties Union* what they are doing to their Church, they would be fired. Yet Church authority dawdled. Nineteen years passed before the Bishops terminated Charles Curran's license to teach contraception at their own university, and ten years before the Jesuits moved the pro-abortion Robert Drinan, S.J., out of Congress. As long as such causes are legitimated by their acceptance within Catholic structures as options, what they represent become "probable opinions" for the faithful.

Unfortunately, the Church, under those circumstances and playing by secular rules, is bound to lose. For example, "academic freedom unbound," a political concept pure and simple, provides whatever leeway society or an institution chooses to allow in order to achieve its purposes. Harvard is secular. It lacks a Cathedral; its house of religion is a Pantheon. All gods are welcome; no god is honored. If a body of Jesuits somehow took over Harvard's theology department — to teach the Hebrew God, Christ as his only Son, and the Catholic Church as the true Church — and Sunday Mass on the university campus were to become the university's highlight of the week, the Company of Jesus would be no more in Cambridge.

As long as Catholic institutions — or the Church — play by rules comfortable to Harvard's agnostics, the faith of Catholicity will be subverted among its own and be an oddity to other Americans. Equally serious is the failure of the Church to take its battle with secularism to the airwaves. Marshall MacLuhan laid down the ABC's of electronic communication: "the medium is the message." Although the so-called "Christian Right" has proved itself more capable of defending its evangelical flock media-wise, Catholics have done poorly in witnessing its gospel message on marriage and family life. Until that effect is remedied, priests like Father Harvey are engaged in an uphill struggle and stand somewhat alone.

Learning About Homosexuals

The homosexual lobby would have Americans believe that they are homophobes, that they are afraid of men who have sex with men. The fact is that most Americans do not know a single homosexual, would not recognize one if they saw him, or at least did not give the subject a second thought until activists for that cause tried to convince the country that "some people are born homosexual." Granted the vagaries of nature in the raw — Siamese twins being but only one example — few Americans would ever designate same sex orgasms as natural. Mankind, by simple observation or shared experience, universally agrees that man and woman were created to copulate with each other, and that the mechanisms of masculinity and femininity are structured for use by heterosexuals only. Men and women have misused their sexual faculties from time immemorial, as they have their other powers, without perpetrators claiming special privileges or protections for their particular behavior. In the Catholic moral tradition, sins against the Sixth Commandment are categorized as *"secundum naturam"* (e.g., adultery) or *"contra naturam."* Sodomy or rectal coition has always been called *"contra naturam"* and against common sense, i.e., obscene.

The fact that the homosexual way of life has achieved a certain acceptable minority status in American society, in government, in public law (even in marriage cases), in media, and in schools does not mean liberation or endorsement of this way of life. It merely illustrates how far our culture has departed from its Judaeo-Christian roots and how little "One Nation Under God" means anymore. The early Mattucine and Bilitis causes grew into so-called "gay activism" when the media made much of the anguish of people forced to live in a closet because they dared not show their faces, as if anguish justified sodomy any more than it does adultery or euthanasia. But, since the Sangerites were successful in selling contraception as a way to end "unwanted pregnancies," the "gays" hoped to gain success with a similar strategy of claiming suffering and discrimination.

Priests of my generation grew up in the tenement quarters of America's large cities. In New York (1916-1936) five hundred school age children filled every neighborhood street at three o'clock in the afternoon, daily and all summer, yet we never saw a homosexual or a pederast. (Indeed no one in "our gang" ever saw a contraceptive until one fell from the pocket of a ball-playing pal, at twenty years old. We were relieved that he was a Protestant!) This new priest spent fifteen years from 1942 onward, in the same neighborhood, around the same tenements, with the same angels in dirty faces and their hardworking fathers and overburdened mothers, yet never saw or heard or received a complaint about a homosexual. We dealt with adultery and masturbation, even a rare lonely abortion, but never was there talk about boys molesting boys sexually — or a man trying it. In 1960 Cardinal Spellman sent me to a fancy neighborhood in the Bronx, where there were two-family homes newly bought at high prices and young upwardly mobile Catholics trying to survive away from the tenement world downtown. One day two policemen reported at the rectory door that they had just arrested two pederasts apparently working the streets regularly during those hours when young children played without supervision. The mothers were at work, too.

This innocence-at-home did not mean that New York City was *Fantasy Land,* not even for naïve priest-types. At the beginning of our college years, a few eighteen-year olds made pocket money delivering dry-cleaned suits and dresses to the penthouses and duplexes in a posh East River area. The Jewish tailor warned them to be careful — that they might run afoul of homosexual seducers. And occasionally they did, payment for delivery being made standing over a marble table on which was arrayed the most disgusting pornography one could envisage. In those days, the approach of a potential pederast was subtle perhaps, still likely to be told by one growing Catholic boy that his naked display was disgusting! Forty years later the police would inform the pastor of the same area that cops dared not enter a "singles" bar in his parish alone, so violent was the conduct they might encounter. Fifty years later, still, two teenage sons of my parishioners — doing the well-remembered delivery work — died of AIDS.

The Political Game

In the mid-fifties the word "homosexuality" almost disappeared from the *New York Times Subject Index.* In 1960 there were only three cross-references found there. By 1964 the entries filled a column of fine print. A few years later homosexuals were staging "sit-in" demonstrations at bars that refused their patronage, writing frank novels, producing plays, and having their lifestyle portrayed on network television programs.

Such political power did not come by happenstance. Some of this power comes from their money. Historically, homosexuals have been identified with specific well-paying occupations and industries. Once content to keep their personal tastes to themselves, even while earning notable salaries in a heterosexual world, they had begun to exert an ever-widening impact on American sexual values by the 1970s. With the help of the media, especially women's magazines, their positions as couturiers, photographers, fashion writers and advertisers enabled unisex to become an acceptable fashion and the purse a male accessory in places like Greenwich Village. In recent years actors complained that many theatrical agents are homosexual and large areas of the theater and film industry are dominated by them. They have also entered the world of scholarship especially in medicine, psychology and sociology. Scholarly books and articles mostly sympathetic to their condition have multiplied.

The scientific question will hardly ever be answered to everyone's satisfaction, not excluding homosexuals in political life, because the evidence on one side or the other of this particular controversy will never be all in at any given time. New data will likely be contradicted by research studies to follow. While this process of investigation goes on, and knowledge about homosexuality, its causes and cures, continues to multiply, people will continue to make moral judgments. These are the judgments which became the unspoken assumptions underlying political positions. The more fundamental question therefore remains: Can overt homosexual conduct be justified morally?

The Moral Question

Can an overt homosexual lifestyle, involving the genital expression of friendship or companionship, be considered a morally acceptable form of human behavior? The question here is not whether a particular homosexual act involves sin. As most Catholics know, the factors which diminish guilt, indeed exculpate the sinner before God, are many. Christ told the Jews: "You justify yourself in the eyes of men, but God reads your heart" (Luke 16:15). Neither does the question apply to the homosexual state, which may be acquired, as other conditions are acquired, without or with little formal sin. Sins are wrongful acts, not states. States may predispose people to do wrong, but they are not identical with wrong. Nor does this question, of itself, say anything about the homosexual's membership in an ecclesial community or about his reception of the sacraments. Religious affiliation and religious practice involve saints and sinners of all descriptions. In the Catholic Church, the confessional is one instrument of support and reconciliation for a large variety of people who occasionally or regularly, in small ways or large, find themselves in situations or engaged in activities which are wrong. Sin, as used here, means a condition or behavior opposed to the known will of God, whom good Catholics are trying to worship effectively and whom presumptively they are trying to please.

When therefore the question is asked — are sexual acts performed by members of the same sex wrong? — the answer must deal only with the needs, not with the person as such, not with his subjective state, not with his position in the Church. If this real distinction between the human person and his behavior is unaccepted, it becomes impossible to have rational discourse on this subject. Whether or not his conduct is good or bad, a human person has intrinsic value. On the other hand, certain conduct of men or women is immoral, harmful to the misbehaving person, and at times disruptive to the common welfare of society. Living together requires general agreement among the people involved on the values and enforceable behavior necessary for them to live together in peace. Otherwise, how can society remain orderly? Hence, whether one begins with a moral principle or a moral judgment, the two questions must be considered separately.

Today, however, under the influence of situation ethics, so-called, the real distinction of moral theology has become blurred. Moral theology is that branch of "the science of God" which, under the guidance of the Church, establishes norms of behavior required by a religious commitment. These norms are more or less probable, giving leeway to believers in the choices they make (e.g., the conditions for a just war). Idolatry and adultery are clear examples of absolutely forbidden behavior always and everywhere. Pastoral theology, on the other hand, starts with a person, not with a principle. Its object is "shepherding" a Catholic toward the better love and service of God. Shepherding can be a slow and delicate process, especially if the person is involved in a seriously sinful state or habit, and regular reception of the sacraments is considered essential to spiritual recovery. Pastoral theology is more of an art than a science. The "shepherd" encourages and supports the struggling penitent; or, for the same pastoral reasons, he may remonstrate with him, or even deny ritual help or sacramental support to a recalcitrant or a contumacious sinner. The Good Shepherd never confuses compassion for a person with condoning evil. At times Christ verbally scourged evildoers, and St. Paul would hardly receive a favorable press today, if he called New Yorkers what he once called Romans, namely, men

> ... filled with every kind of wickedness, maliciousness, greed, ill will, envy, murder, bickering, deceit, craftiness. They are gossips and slanderers, they hate God, are insolent, haughty, boastful, ingenious in their

wrongdoing and rebellious toward their parents. One sees in them men without conscience, without loyalty, without affection, without pity. They know God's just decree that all who do such things deserve death; they not only do them but approve them in others. (Rom. 1:28-32)

Fr. John Harvey, who has written more on the morality of homosexuality than any other American theologian, believes quite correctly that "pastoral *ad hoc* solutions which ignore the objective immorality of homosexual acts would reduce our sexual ethics to personalistic shambles." Still some Catholic theologians have been moving precisely in that direction, following the lead of Joseph Fletcher, "that anything and everything is right or wrong according to the situation."

Whenever the teaching Church has been asked the question of whether an overt homosexual lifestyle, involving the genital expression of affection, can be considered a morally acceptable form of human behavior, the answer has been a consistent and resounding "No." From the earliest Christian days, homosexual acts, like murder and adultery, have been considered *clamantia peccata*, sins crying to heaven. Nowhere in the Bible or Talmud, in the writings of the Fathers or Doctors of the Church, in any official statement by any Church authority, is there any suggestion that human sexuality has been intended by nature or by God for use by members of the same sex. Both the Torah and the Talmud condemned homosexuality, sometimes with legal severity: "If a man lies with a male as with a woman, both of them shall be put to death for their abominable deed" (Lev. 20:13).

While it is customary to dismiss these Old Testament legalisms as time-conditioned Jewish mores rather than divine moralisms, the early Christian Church itself did not look kindly on homosexual practices, in part because these were expressions of Greco-Roman licentiousness, which among the upper classes included pederasty. In the middle second century, Justin the Martyr reported cases of boys bought and trained especially for this lifestyle by their own kinsmen. The general revulsion of the early Christians was most vigorously expressed by Paul, who railed against the Romans that they, who should have known God through his created things, fashioned instead gods of their own who would not interfere with their perverse desires and because of this wickedness:

> God delivered them up to disgraceful passions. Their women exchanged natural intercourse for unnatural, and the men gave up natural intercourse with women and burned with lust for one another. Men did shameful

things with men, and thus received in their own persons the penalty for their perversity. (1:26-27)

Paul is even more specific in his first letter to the Corinthians, who were reverting to sexual depravity six years after their conversion, including religious prostitution, one of the characteristics of pagan life. He reminds them that their bodies are members of Christ, temples of the Holy Spirit, to be used for the glory of God. Once upon a time they engaged in sexual debauchery, he recalls, but those days are gone:

> Do not deceive yourselves: no fornicators, idolaters, misers, no Sodomites, thieves, or drunkards, no slanderers or robbers will inherit God's Kingdom. Such were some of you: but you have been washed, consecrated, justified in the name of our Lord Jesus Christ. (6:9-11)

No serious student of Christian theology reading this passage can explain away this stern reminder as not central to the moral code for Christians. Sodomistic sexual acts, including homosexual ones, are condemned simply and absolutely as characteristic of a pagan way of life, certainly not the way of Christ.

St. Thomas Aquinas is one other who, like the authors of Scripture, held firm ideas on homosexuality. In his judgment, the most sacred of all human relational acts is man's intercourse with God, a subject upon which God has a good deal to say through revelation and through the way he made human nature. Aquinas was not an innovator in this matter. He handed on the consistent Christian tradition going back to the very origins of the Church. The condemnation of homosexual practices of early Christian Gnostics, the assertions of Lactantius, of Clement of Alexandria, of Augustine, and of the Penitential Books echoed one of the few moral norms that can be called part of revealed doctrine. The Angelic Doctor, interpreting Paul, argued that human nature, with its divinely created male and female components, ordains sexuality toward the well-being of the human race. For him the "right reason" for sexuality was the pairing of marriage and the procreation of a family. Were he speaking in popular contemporary parlance, he might say: Take a good look at male and female and ask what other purpose there could be in such a divine intervention, other than marriage and family life.

Aquinas goes on further to insist that harmony of man with God demands such respect for the order of nature that vices which violate the right reasons of nature are to be abominated. He supports the stern judgment of Augustine in his *Confessions:*

> Those foul offenses that are against nature should be everywhere and at all times detested and punished, such as were those people of Sodom, which should all nations commit, they should all stand guilty of the same crime, by the law of God which had not made man that they should so abuse one another. (III:8)

And because acts of these kinds are so opposed to "things as determined by nature," they are "most grave and shameful," deserve to be called "unnatural vices" and are the gravest sins of all, graver than even incest and adultery, even rape.

The Second Vatican Council, a thousand years later, had only two short paragraphs on "sin," leaving some badly taught Catholics at the parish level to say, as is sometimes said, that love and compassion have replaced sin and guilt as Catholic staples. They do not realize, thinking this, that they also redefine Christ and the salvific nature of the Paschal Mystery. Certain new theologians, in an attempt to justify homosexual acts, have constructed their own ethical norms: "Be yourself; realize your possibilities." But by now it must be clear that however much sense relativism makes to the humanist, it flies in the face of a clear and consistent line of reasoning that goes right back through the time of Christ to religious Jews. Vatican II was very clear on the centrality of sexuality to family life:

> All those who exercise influence over communities and social groups should work efficiently for the welfare of marriage and the family. Public authority should regard it as a sacred duty to recognize, protect, and promote their authentic nature, to shield public morality, and to favor the prosperity of domestic life. *(Gaudium et Spes, 52)*

Consequently, most Catholic authorities, regardless of what school of theology they prefer, maintain to this day that overt homosexual acts are seriously wrong and have no place in any Christian scheme of sexual life.

Government as Moralist

Should the power of government — including public censure or civil penalties — be used against employers, landlords, and public officials of one kind or another who refuse to hire, rent or provide requested services to homosexuals? Should government be authorized to engage in educational activity which has as its ultimate objective branding anti-homosexual judgments, opinions, and activity as prejudice, intolerance, or bigotry? Should government help create a climate of tolerance, if not approval, of the homosexual lifestyle? By what process shall the right answers to these questions be decided, and who shall decide?

Those who see no harm in homosexual activity are inclined to answer all questions one way; those who look upon such behavior as a serious human aberration and a danger to society, are likely to answer them quite differently. Between the extremes are a variety of opinions, more reflective of class than religious preference.

Central to any political discussion of "gay rights" is the word "discrimination," a term which in contemporary secular society has become an emotion-packed word. Discrimination suggests, for example, that no Black or Brown need apply for an opening in a job, a house, or a camp because certainly there will be no opening, even if the Black or Brown man is qualified, respectable and can pay his way. Years ago both Catholics and Jews faced those same unfriendly and debilitating judgments by people with that kind of power to say no. To protect helpless minorities from this kind of treatment, the power of government was finally brought to bear on their behalf. Blacks and Browns were forced thereby into jobs, housing, and camps for several reasons: (1) under law Blacks and Catholics were as good as Whites and Protestants; (2) their economic and social disabilities were total and pervasive, and if allowed to continue, the danger of social rebellion was present; (3) and decades of voluntary effort to gain public acceptance of these minority groups had failed. Prior to such civil rights legislation, Blacks were still Pullman porters or shoeshine boys.

Although there are still complaints on both sides of the issue, crusades on the part of these new minorities have been, for the most part, relatively successful. The ensuing results merited the approval or acquiescence of the electorate and justified the limitations on other people's freedom which government intervention implied. If civil rights legislation compelled people to work or live with people for whom they had no liking or appetite, and forced leaders of business, education, or social welfare to revise their management procedures, sometimes at high economic cost, the end result was to improve the class position and the economic level of these minorities, and to demonstrate in a public way that as far as the nation is concerned there is nothing second-class about being Black, Catholic or a woman. Not everyone agrees with this judgment, especially those who decry the growing power of government over the private lives of citizens or the misuse of that power, and by 1990 a backlash against reverse discrimination was well underway. Nonetheless, civil rights legislation has still generally upheld a moderate degree of human progress, although its amendment to prevent "quotas" is likely.

The political question now to be asked is this: Does the extension of government force to protect and promote "gay rights" have the same justification? Further, would such enforced guarantee of gay rights also be judged social progress? And, is it likely that the general public will validate such judgments? Organizations which consider themselves humanistic usually give affirmative answers to all three questions; conservative thinkers tend to say "not so." However, Michael Novak, an otherwise considered liberal spokesman, poses this objection:

> To call a proposal "progressive" or "radical" does not save it from being regressive. Most evils do present themselves in the guise of moral goodness. "Gay liberation" is not a form of genuine liberation, not a form of human progress. It is one more false god, one more false prophesy, against which it is our vocation to offer the dignity of resistance. (*Commonweal*, 31 May 1974)

Consequently, the definition of "discrimination" is important to this political discussion. It is expected that every cultured person will be discriminating — which means being a person of good judgment. Current fashion, however, says that no person should discriminate at any time. Yet, one synonym for discrimination is "discernment," the person of discernment being highly prized, presumptively having the ability to make the right kinds of distinctions, a quality essential for one with good judgment. People of sense, all of them, discriminate all the time; that is, they judge for themselves what is good for them personally or for their group. Republicans discriminate against Democrats, Americans with or without Senator McCarthy discriminated against Communists, and in spite of Vatican II, Catholic bishops do not seem to be ordaining women. In making such judgments, most people pursue their own best interests, which means they are more for themselves than they are against others. Many of their judgments will exclude sharing something with an out-group and will be considered necessary to protect them against a threat or an enemy. Choices such as these are not bad, and they may indeed be good discriminating judgments, important for self-esteem, for identity, and for self-protection. It should be clear after Watergate that if no man is an island, he nonetheless needs some of his own private worlds kept sacred against public prying or public compulsion toward total conformity to someone else's standard for living.

It follows, therefore, that "discrimination" becomes bad only when the judgment is bad. Usually this will be somebody else's bad judgment. In a society which values freedom but not its malicious exercise, one party's judgment may represent discernment of the highest order while his neighbor's may be viewed as the basest form of discrimination. The winner in the battle of ethical assumptions or preferable freedom is most frequently determined in the free marketplace of ideas and associations, with losers allowed to sulk in the circle of more congenial friends. Government rarely arbitrates the rightness or wrongness of people's judgments until some mass injury is being inflicted, when all other efforts at rescue have failed and as significant dangers loom to threaten the social order.

On this basis, one is entitled to ask the following subsidiary questions: Are "gays" the exact legal and political counterpart of "Blacks, Hispanics, Italians, Jews and women?" Even if gayhood is considered a neutral political bloc, as sex and race and religion are *per se,* what special entitlements in nature belong to homosexuals, and what social disabilities are being inflicted on homosexuals which require the special protection of public law and government agencies? Finally, if homosexuality is more than merely cultural deviance and is really pathology, what are the ultimate implications of gay legislation for society, for the family structures of society, for those against whom it may be used, and for gays themselves?

In response to the first question, gayhood is being given constitutional status, as if it were in the class of manhood or womanhood. Without question, the Constitution accords all Americans the right *to be* anything they want. The homosexual state of being would not have concerned the Founding Fathers. The differences between gayhood and manhood/womanhood are significant, certainly as far as national ethos is concerned, a national ethos originally formed not only by the Constitution but by the public law, by public mores, and by the Ten Commandments. Manhood/womanhood is the natural condition of a majority of the citizenry, homosexuality the deviant tendency of a minuscule proportion. Manhood/womanhood is supported and protected by an extensive code of law because men as fathers and women as mothers are essential to family life, children, and national character. No society, not even pre-Christian Greece, whose vast majority was heterosexually married but whose poets and dramatists idealized pederasty, ever endorsed or encouraged homosexuality.

There is so little evidence of homosexual cells among the poor and so much visible evidence of their presence in the choicest residential areas of any large metropolitan area, that a better case would have to be made for government intervention on the behalf of people well able to take care of their own interests, perhaps better than many heterosexuals.

On the other hand, the implications of government intervention are far-reaching. For government to insert itself into private human relations without evidence of a demonstrable need is a departure from standard legal practice. Government bodies in the nineteenth century, which never intervened on behalf of Catholics and Jews, waited one hundred years to do so for workingmen and Blacks, and only now are acting on behalf of women.

In the absence of that justification, such intervention limits the freedom of citizens to make judgments about their own affairs and according to their own norms of judgment. For example, employers, homeowners, labor leaders, educators and others have the right — in the absence of any law to the contrary — to consider morals or lifestyles in the selection of those who work or live with them.

Government intervention preempts the valid and proper work of gay activist groups to educate the general citizenry concerning the more egregious violations of decency and fair play for the homosexual. Gay organizations have every political right to propagate their cause and, correctly done, this can lead to greater understanding and tolerance, if not total acceptance. In the United States, however, government sanctions are reserved for support of activities and groups demonstrably vital to the nation's common good. Can this be said of homosexuals?

Government legislation of the type currently proposed flows not out of some popular mandate, clearly perceived at least in the making, but simply out of fear of a minority pressure group, which by its aggressive tactics has frightened the political leadership in some large cities, even if the number of votes deliverable in return are negligible. Such a precedent for lawmaking is not desirable.

Without demonstrable justification, "gay rights" bills, following the pattern of other civil rights legislation, will lead to *de facto* quota systems and reverse discrimination sanctioned by law. How does one "prove" discrimination? By pointing to the scarcity of homosexuals in homes, organizations, schools, and camps. To purge oneself of discrimination one will be required to spend a great deal of time before city agencies or in court, the end result of which will be to overcompensate by "reverse discrimination" or by demographic movement to areas where these compulsions do not apply.

Finally, there is the symbolism of the law itself, a not inconsiderable aspect of all legislation, which besides commanding or forbidding action, is one of society's greatest educational tools. There is no question that civil rights legislation, given to Blacks, not only has opened new economic and educational opportunities to them but has provided a certain amount of respectability and respect to those who have used the openings well. The results are not even, nor all in, and many may never be perfectly satisfying to Blacks. But if Black is not beautiful to all Whites, it certainly is far more acceptable than in 1954, a development which may not lead to a Brown American race, but does promise growing homogeneous relationships and some browning. Without question, gay activists wish to use public laws to demand the hiring of "models" of homosexuality on the staffs of public and private institutions. Conversely, laws governing criminality, pornography, abortion, and the administration thereof have led to a general acceptance or tolerance of all three conditions. Is this general acceptance of homosexuality as an alternative lifestyle what the public really wants? From a study of the literature, one gathers the impression that society will become more democratic if all taboos are removed. But it also becomes clear that the political attitude depends on what taboos are being discussed. One psychiatrist reminded his readership that were all taboos lifted, most humans would be functioning bisexuals so that "pathology might very well consist of exclusive interest in one sex, regardless of which sex one chooses."

A good number of unproven but not necessarily true or equally true statements have been made about what may or may not happen if "gays" were successfully to achieve equal status, equal recognition, or equal rights. On the one hand, gays are not likely to take over the sexual world, even of the young, since homosexuality is a self-defeating condition, which gays would not want passed on to their own children, presuming they had any. On the other hand, homosexuality, being an unhappy state for most, even for those who have no moral opinions on the matter, ought not to be given by public law that which it cannot gain by private effort, the status of a respectable sexual option. Society ought to have laws which, whatever else they do, symbolize its own basic values. As of this moment, some laws symbolize strange values — prurience, dishonesty, disregard for marriage, for life. Nonetheless, since family life (a heterosexual experience) is essential to the well-being of the nation, those engaged in family life ought not to be encumbered with more cultural difficulties than necessary. In other words, they should be allowed to presume for themselves and their children that heterosexual mating and the education of children to be heterosexual is the right and proper thing to do, without having public institutions saying even implicitly that this is not necessarily so.

Fr. John Harvey, O.S.F.S.

By the time Father Harvey received the go-ahead from Cardinal Cooke in 1980 to undertake *Courage* in the Archdiocese of New York, the American Church was deep into a serious homosexual problem. The scandal was slow in coming to the surface, although priests of an older generation could hardly believe it even when it did arrive. During the 1970's, homosexual candidates were appearing in major seminaries, even on faculty, harassing heterosexuals, too, by labeling them homophobes. As the decade progressed, metropolitan newspapers, such as the *Milwaukee Sentinel,* were writing of widespread homosexuality among priests and about the court cases initiated by parents against priests for pederasty. *Dignity*, a pro-homosexual lobby, found a favorable home in many dioceses. Pastors provided special, sometimes illicit, Sunday liturgies for homosexuals in various places, much to the chagrin of bishops, some of whom were intimidated, others of whom demanded the offenders to cease and desist under threat of canonical sanction. The Church may have large room in her embrace for sinners during their fall and recovery, but revolutionary groups organized to crucify the Church for her teaching are to be seen as wicked and are to be treated as wicked (cf. Mt. 24:45-51).

Into this moral morass came Fr. Harvey's *Courage,* an unusual but apt name for a body of men and women dedicated to finding, recovering or maintaining virtue in their lives. The quest for the state of grace is a normal, not spectacular, attribute of Christian faith, but in a secular culture it is likely to be as much an object of scorn or punishment, as it was for Christ. *Courage* was founded in the Canon Cardijn mold — an apostolate of "like to like," small groups meeting to intensify their faith, to develop piety, and to engage in activity among and for homosexuals with a view to their spiritual well-being. *Courage* is a "spiritual support system" more than a program of psychic uplift. Emotional benefits follow, to be sure, as they do in *Daytop* and in *Alcoholics Anonymous*. These earlier exercises of "reality therapy" were far more successful in curing bad habits of addiction than the psychic bloodletting associated with Sigmund Freud.

What *A.A.* and *Daytop* did for alcoholics and addicts — and even what Annie Sullivan did for Helen Keller — Fr. Harvey undertook to do for would-not-be-homosexuals, on the sound principle that good learning is the end result of good teaching. If the road to hell was paved with good intentions, *Courage* aimed to build a road to virtue graced with authentic Catholic structures.

Courage faced an unusual first problem, namely to restore the faith of its members in the Church's teaching on homosexuality. The presumption that Catholics "have that mind which is in Christ Jesus" (Phil. 2:5) is no longer valid. If those homosexually-inclined (for any reason) were to act Catholic, they had to think Catholic. It was bad enough that the secular culture of its nature was sexually seductive, but so were important instruments of Catholic misinformation. In hindsight, who can believe that the theological brains of the episcopal conference — *The Catholic Theological Society of America* — published in 1977 the results of its five years research into *Human Sexuality,* and disseminated these gems through the Catholic body:

> Scripture is not concerned with sexuality as such. (31)
>
> Mate-swapping is not ideal ... [but] the final word on this subject has not been said. (149)
>
> There may occasionally arise exceptions" to fidelity and marriage. (151)
>
> Premarital intercourse may be justified if it represents a "loving relationship." (166)
>
> Bestiality is pathological "when heterosexual outlets are available." (230)

This is what *Human Sexuality* had to say about homosexuality (214-215): "Homosexuals have the same right to love, intimacy and relationships as heterosexuals .... and to receive communion, too.

This *vade mecum* of "progressive" Catholic renewal even received praise from the *New York Times* (July 7, 1997) because "the values for which it speaks owes much to humanist psychology." And so did the catechesis in many Catholic centers.

Once *Courage* members passed over the hurdle of "right thinking," they faced Fr. Harvey's second demand that they commit themselves to a life of chastity. They are not asked to forsake the comfort they find in the company of men, only to love their single state, see it as their vocation, mortify their sexual urges, and avoid the occasions of sin. These are the ordinary Church expectations for all single Catholics, especially when exposed to temptation. Homosexuals, however, face double jeopardy in the bad example of fellow Catholics and through the widespread dissent in Catholic publications on matters sexual. Still, *Courage* sought to serve as a cloister where souls in communion with a priest and friends gain confidence in their ability to be practicing Catholics. Of course, their regular participation in the Eucharistic liturgy and the sacramental/devotional life of the Church is Fr. Harvey's third step toward recovery.

Does *Courage* work? For those who are faithful to the program, yes. Critics dismiss it as unrealistic and an insignificant therapy relative to the wide scope of today's homosexual activity. A group like *Dignity* draws larger numbers since it is supportive of what is called responsible homosexual behavior. Somehow, in that school of revised Christian thought, permanent homosexual relationships are more virtuous than the casual, although neither way of life enjoys the favor of the Church or of Christ. Certainly he who labeled "lust for a woman" as adultery (Mt. 5:28) would not look kindly on lust for a man, even if it were enduring. What casuistry bearing the name Christian would have Christ really present in the Eucharist coexist with someone who lives in serious sin? The sinner may be invincibly ignorant, and so before God stands excused; but in the present era of pervasive communication, the chances are that those who consciously do not see sodomy as sin, really do not see Christ as the Son of God.

Fr. Harvey stands with John Paul II as a "voice crying in the wilderness." He works in a post-Christian era, when those who insist that everyone must hug each other before the *Agnus Dei*, or at least must picket for peace or racial justice because bishops encourage those things, but refuse to take advice from bishops about what to do in bed. The founder of *Courage* is a beacon of small light in a culture where "right thinking" about sex is an embarrassment, and he pays a price for believing what the Church teaches. He also subsists in a Catholic community where elites place more stock in the guesswork of behavioral science and opinion research than they do in Scripture or the teaching office of the Church. He is a chaplain of a lay apostolate, the kind which has had little long-lived success anywhere, usually because of bad judgments by priests who are cowered by entrenched views of secular society, or by its power-brokers who promise to do damage to those who contest its vision of human destiny.

God's Word on sex, better known as the Sixth Commandment, underpins marriage "till death do us part" and the family as the cornerstone of every nation. Seculars like to forget that Judaeo-Christianity created an entire civilization built on all Ten of the Commandments. Today, Christians are engaged by a godless civilization, one founded on the unconditioned will of the people and their free choice uninhibited by God's law — with antisocial consequences visible everywhere. How strange, is it not, that post-Vatican II reformers readily forgot that the Council, addressing the difficulties of the modern world *(Gaudiun et Spes),* named "atheism" up front as "one of the most serious problems of our times" and one which "believers can have more than a little to do with [its] rise." Bishops overlooked this warning, too. The life of the Sixth Commandment would not be gasping for breath had bishops realized that the fight over contraception was not over the unwanted babies of mothers who already had a few, or if they realized the inexorable link between the condom and an abortionist's needle, or between an annulment and an annulment mill. What bishop at Council's end dreamed that he would knowingly ordain a homosexual priest ever?

The tragic fact is that the Sixth Commandment is no longer the big issue in or out of the Catholic community. The Church can nit-pick about sexual matters all she wants — on partial birth abortion, for example — but the assumption on which she bases her Christian case are unbelieved, even by leading Jesuits. The divinity of Christ and the Fatherhood of God are now in doubt as far as American public policy about family life and sexual behavior is concerned. This involves a very substantial confrontation of secular society with Christianity and will not really be faced by the gentlemanly side-bar discussions of Catholic clerics with the priesthood of an omnicompetent godless State. Equally important is the question: Are Catholics themselves still siding with God against Mammon?

More than once John Paul II, looking at the present crisis, has said, "We must begin all over again." Not long ago, Cardinal Joseph Ratzinger mourned how the Catholic faith "means less" today.

Back in the 19th century when America's ethos was Christian and Protestant, and when the issue in public dispute was not God or Christ but the Pope, or the potential takeover of the country by Catholics,

American bishops used their cathedral pulpits and parish halls to speak of Christ's divinity, eternal life, the immortality of the soul, and papal infallibility. The main issue in the secular crusade is the existence of God and the place of the Decalogue in the country's life, and we hear little of those cosmic issues in the public square.

Back in 1845, Orestes Brownson, the country's first intellectual convert, made this comment on the godless democracy he saw aborning then:

> The people are assumed to be what almighty God is to the universe, the first cause, the medial cause, the final cause. It emanates from them; it is administered by them; and, moreover, they are to keep watch and provide for its right administration.

Then, this reformer Unitarian minister expanded his concern:

> It is a beautiful theory, and would work admirably, if it were not for one little difficulty, namely, the people are fallible, both individually and collectively, and governed by their passions and interests which not infrequently lead them far astray and produce much mischief. The government must necessarily follow their will; and whenever that will happens to be blinded by passion, or misled by ignorance or interest, the government must inevitably go wrong without doing injustice.

Brownson conceded that the country needed religion to deal with this inevitability, "a religion," he said, "which is above the people and controls them, or it will not answer the purpose." In his view, once the supreme civil magistrate also becomes the sovereign pontiff of religion, "religion and the Church, if disobedient to his will, are to be turned out of house and home, or dragooned into submission." And so, he became a Roman Catholic.

Strangely, the Catholic Church is being defined by some of her own as "people religion," not the Body of Christ. Doors through the protective walls of her Catholic faith, however narrow they are by design (Mt. 7:13-14), have been left ajar by hirelings and foes of that faith already inside. One of the wider doors reads "The Sixth Commandment," the way out of which Christ said was an "easy" one and which "leads to destruction" (cf. Mt. 7:13-14). Fr. John Harvey stands at the Church's door as a John the Baptist, and as a watchman for his portion of God's people. Every so often he looks over his shoulder hoping that the Savior has arrived.

Chapter Six

Waiting for Grace:

The Pastoral Care of Those Who Are Not Yet Disposed to Follow the Commandments

Rev. BENEDICT GROESCHEL, C.F.R.

The thorny problem of the pastoral care of those who desire to participate in the life of the Church, and who are yet either unwilling or unable to observe its moral teachings, is one that many pastors and pastoral workers encounter every day. In every good-sized parish there are people beginning to experience a real call to conversion, but who are involved in moral difficulties ranging from invalid marriages and homosexual relationships to addiction to alcohol and drugs. There are others who are unaware of the call to real conversion but who at least want to be a part of the life of the Church, and this desire may indeed be a call of divine grace.

The question of the pastoral care of this very needy group presents itself over and over again. What can be done for them without becoming an enabler, someone who out of compassion or need to be agreeable or even guilt, cooperates in another person's immorality or psychological confusion by pretending that a real and ongoing conversion has taken place?

When I thought of writing an article as a tribute to Fr. John Harvey OSFS, my friend and colleague of twenty-five years, I could think of no more appropriate question to address than this one, because the loyal, intelligent and productive elements of his life for over 50 years as a priest has been related precisely to this issue. Long before anyone else apparently even thought of it, Fr. Harvey had become a true and loyal spiritual father and guide to many struggling with homosexual tendencies and orientation who wanted to lead an authentic Christian life. In fact, when the Servant of God, Terence Cardinal Cooke asked me to find a priest to begin an apostolate with homosexually-oriented Catholics who wanted to lead a devout and chaste life, I said immediately to him "Let's try to get Father Harvey." Thus began the movement that the pioneer members named "Courage." To express my own deep regard for Father Harvey, I chose to examine this difficult topic. Even though I realize I'm exploring turbulent waters, I will do so, and leave myself open to correction, which I welcome.

The Wait for Grace

My own lifelong meditations on the *Confessions* of St. Augustine and his other writings have made me aware that the call to conversion does not necessarily come as a "bolt out of the blue", as it did to St. Paul. Most frequently it is a gradual call, a summons of grace that occurs in often painful steps. Augustine recalls: "I twisted and turned on my chain ... and you, O Lord, redoubled the stings of Your mercy." There is a time of painful ambiguity between the initial dissatisfaction of individuals with their sinful state and the step of accepting God's will manifested in Scripture, moral tradition and the teaching of the Church. Augustine describes this state of mind very well. Since the whole Christian life is in itself a series of conversions, leading one ever closer to God, we should all be familiar with this pain and ambiguity. Devout persons with no serious sins at all, will become more and more dissatisfied with their own habitual lack of charity, prayerfulness or humility. These people will also long to "leap up and break free" with the help of God. But in the case where a person is bound by a seriously sinful habit of behavior — Augustine calls it "the iron chain of habit" — there are important pastoral problems that must be addressed.

To receive the sacraments as a vital member of the Mystical Body of Christ, a person must be "in the state of grace," that is without any deliberate serious moral fault, any mortal sin intruding into their relationship with God and blocking the flow of divine grace. The concept of the state of grace, which was very clear to believers only thirty years ago, has become obscured by many factors, all of them, to my way of thinking, dangerous to one's spiritual welfare: moral relativism, subjectivism, theological and moral ignorance, the subtle acceptance of pagan or hedonistic values, the sexual revolution and sloppy pastoral practices. "If you love me, keep my commandments" has been replaced with "Try it, you 'll. like it" and doing it "my own way."

Since we are considering here the question of homosexuality, let me begin by stating my own conviction that homosexuals should not be singled out as those most responsible for the moral mess in which our culture finds itself. This charge is often laid at their door by others. The retreat from moral values began in the early 1960's, at a time when homosexual people had little direct public influence. Moral relativism with its intended moral collapse is the responsibility of a very wide spectrum of society, including clergy of many denominations, who rather dumbly went along for the ride, or better, the slide down the slippery slope. The list of issues is too long, but just for openers, we could mention the acceptance of public pornography in the entire media, the acceptance of pre-marital sexual behavior, promiscuity, infidelity to marriage and religious vows, and the acceptance of the whole contraceptive mentality, leading to the legal sanction of abortion. Although the noisy members of the gay sub-culture usually support all of the above, so do a great many other influential groups.

The Church and the Unconverted

The Catholic Church, and in fact, if we are honest, all older denominations beyond the first decades of enthusiasm have always tolerated moral inconsistencies of one kind or another. For instance, despite the absolute condemnation of racial slavery issued by Pope Eugene IV in 1435 when Europeans first met black people in the Canary Islands, and despite the fact that slavery completely contradicted the Gospel and justice itself, a small number of otherwise respectable Catholics in the United States kept slaves. In terms of other more personal sins, members of the Church in the past tolerated alcoholism on a grand scale while every moralist and teacher routinely taught that intoxication was a serious sin. Many a drunk was tolerated for years before anything was said, as in the case of slave owners. There were always effective voices in the Church raised against these damaging moral problems. But one can cite many other examples of tolerance of serious moral lapses, ranging from violence to women and children all the way to simony. This tolerance often hurt great numbers of individuals and families as it did with the case of slavery and alcoholism. And yet in our society tolerance is always seen as a healthy attitude. According to the American College Dictionary tolerance is an attitude of fairness or patience with opinions or behaviors that differ from our own opinions.

Those who had scruples about the tolerance of certain vices often cited our Savior's compassion to justify themselves, although Christ's attitude was not tolerance at all, but rather patience and mercy toward the individual. Christ did not have opinions; He was the Truth. The following illustrative paragraph from *The Moral Teaching of the New Testament* by Rudolph Schnackenburg, one of the most eminent Scripture scholars of our time, sums up very well the attitude of Christ towards the weakness of his followers:

> So then we must let the words of Jesus stand in all their severity and ruggedness. Any mitigation, however well intended, is an attack on his moral mission. But how Jesus judges those who fall short of his demands is quite another matter. His behavior towards the disciples gives us an object-lesson on this point. He took back even Simon Peter, who denied him three times and yet was the leader of the circle of the twelve after Peter had bitterly repented his actions, and he confirmed him in his position as the chief of the disciples and shepherd of the sheep (cf. Luke 22:32; John 21: 15-17). Admonition and mercy are found together. It is the mercy of God which always comes first. It comes definitively into history with the person and works of Jesus. But Jesus also longs to awaken the ultimate powers for good in those laid hold of by the love of God and saved from eternal ruin. They should now thankfully do the holy will of God in its totality, unalloyed. If in spite of everything they again succumb to human weakness and wretchedness, God's mercy will not fail if they turn back in penitence. (p. 881)

Our Divine Savior was not tolerant. He was patient and merciful, and in fact the believer knows that he is patient with us still. No one, even a candidate for canonization, leads a life without faults and sins. The criterion for canonization is not sinlessness but heroic virtue. I was told by those in the Vatican responsible for the canonization process, that if I proved that my candidate, Terence Cardinal Cooke was without sin, I was lying.

A result of moral relativism is a denial of the need for conversion. People speak of a value-free society, and even seem to think of a

Christian life without morality. It is absurd to speak about a society without morality. There are moral faults or sins, many of which no society can tolerate because they threaten its existence. Often this same immoral behavior is more seriously prohibited by the Church. Things as evil as willful murder, and as venial as petty thievery, are still condemned by government and religion as well. This is because they are not only wrong but they threaten good public order.

Our own society seems to be very confused about sexual morality. This is no surprise. The history of sanctions and punishment of sexual misdeeds would make a very interesting study in religious as well as civil inconsistency. Even if one confines this study to the United States in the twentieth century, the inconsistency and changing values and unstable morality would leave one's head spinning. For instance, homosexual acts between consenting adults were criminal behavior in almost every state at the beginning of this century, whereas they could be absolved in confession with only a moderate penance, like perhaps the saying of the rosary. The social taboo against premarital sex was almost universal in the first half of this century, whereas now the great social taboo is smoking cigarettes. Smoking has definitely become a social sin, while fornication is celebrated every day in the media. The majority of homosexually-oriented people will ask: "If sex is OK for everybody else, how come we have to behave and are even asked to lead a life of chastity and sexual abstinence ?" The question is asked not only by members of the "Gay Scene," the large and noisy members of the active homosexual sub-culture, but by quiet, unobtrusive homosexuals, who find parading around with pink balloons at demonstrations and campy activities very distasteful. Some clergy, responding to this question and perhaps dealing with their own conflicts and inconsistencies, openly espouse the gay-lesbian culture, or at least communicate approval rather than pastoral acceptance of the individual, which, in fact, is called for by the Gospel.

Tolerance vs. Acceptance

Tolerance is a poor substitute for acceptance of the individual while keeping the door open to conversion. Acceptance of a person does not imply agreement or approval. It is based on humanity not opinion. In its highest personal form it is an operation of Christian charity. The observable tolerance of what was wrong and sinful in church history is no justification for continuing moral inconsistencies now. The teaching of the Church remained even when the practice failed. It was not the Church that failed, but the people who failed the Church. As the very first Christians, the apostles, failed so badly when they ran away from Christ in the Garden of Gethsemane, I do not have the slightest doubt that many in the Church failed to condemn slavery or alcoholism or many other things that destroyed or undermined family life. They had to repent or at the end of their days to render an account. Their failure may have resulted from an inability to do anything, in which case they were not responsible; or from what might be called weakness of mind and resolution, in which case they are only partially responsible; or from sinful omission out of fear and human respect, in which case they were in fact responsible. But in no case can their tolerance of evil be seen as an act of virtue. In many cases, those who did nothing were victims themselves, like the slaves and the spouses of severe alcoholics or even the alcoholics themselves. They were rarely responsible, although there were courageous souls who took on incredible odds, like Dred Scott, the slave who changed the system, or Bill Wilson, who founded Alcoholics Anonymous.

Inappropriate pastoral tolerance is a special problem all of its own, because being the spiritual shepherd, one must not "break the bruised reed or quench the smoldering flax." It is very easy for a pastoral person to become complacent, to move from tolerance to reluctant acceptance, and then when challenged to suddenly find oneself defending the very evil that was merely tolerable at first. A very sad case in point is the Bishop of Linz, Austria, who had every reason to be deeply opposed to the Nazi's annexation of his country and to their open abuse of the Church. He nonetheless encouraged the conscientious objector, the Servant of God Franz Jagerstatter, to do his duty and "to serve the fatherland' in the Nazi army. St Augustine warned pastors and others in pastoral roles to be careful not to be drawn into evil by becoming hirelings. Pastoral people of all kinds must be truthful in whatever they do. To use the wry remark of St. Gregory the Great, pastors must take care not to become "watch dogs that cannot bark."

The Church and Homosexuality

It is a fact that direct homosexual behavior has been identified as morally wrong for Christians since the beginning. St. Paul condemned it in the Epistle to the Romans (Rom 1:26-27). The moral tradition of the

Church has never veered on this point, although at times people in the Church have moved into pastoral tolerance. Ages like the Renaissance even betray an indulgence. In fact members of the Renaissance Church were often indulgent of many things, but even in those morally disreputable times, there were always those who raised their voices.

The reason for the moral sanctions against direct homosexual acts are many and varied. To contemporary people, unfamiliar with the idea of objective truth, they look like abstract ideas, such as the Natural Law. At this time it is easier to understand objections growing out of the need to protect children and family life. The fact that the vast majority of societies have generated social taboos against homosexual behavior (instinctual and powerful prohibitions), should not be forgotten, although the media in the industrialized (and now decadent) world have carried on a noisy and consistent campaign against the taboo of homosexuality for a quarter of a century.

Nonetheless recent polls have shown that disapproval of homosexuality is still strong in the United States. This is despite the fact that those who express even misgivings about the unqualified acceptance of homosexual behavior are constantly branded as homophobic. The function of such a taboo like the one against homosexuality is not to make life miserable for people who already have problems, but to protect family life and society itself. Often taboos are seen merely as prejudices, but they are essential components of social life. It is astonishing that a social taboo against smoking was generated in the United States in less than twenty years. It must be recalled in discussing the taboo against homosexuality that most people with this orientation have no intention in any way of upsetting the social order or attracting youngsters into a forbidden life. Unfortunately, because of the influence of media, some militant homosexuals have come along and have expressed clearly their intention of upsetting this societal protection of the family. I recall one time at a pro-life march, seeing twenty or thirty teenagers and young adults with pro-gay banners, screaming "we will get your kids!" This kind of behavior should be objectionable to all regardless of sexual orientation, if they have a sense of social and moral consciousness.

Taboo and Morals

It is my impression as a psychologist that many people have some sexual identity conflicts, conscious or unconscious, especially in early adolescence when they may experience an attraction for either sex. Others experience attractions or other behavior that is morally forbidden and/or under a social taboo. The taboo, when operative, pushes the individual toward an appropriate sexual adjustment. It is worth mentioning that the purpose of a societal taboo should not be difficult to identify. Taboos do not emerge from think-tanks. They are not abstract, and they can be irrational. To put it simply, a taboo will generally come forth from the guts of people. It remains to be seen if the somewhat artificially fabricated taboo against smoking will last over the years. (I say this as someone who is absolutely delighted that smoking has gone out as an accepted social convention.)

Although there is a good deal of noisy denial in the gay subculture, a great many homosexually-oriented people, and others with serious sexual identity conflicts of other kinds, will be very explicit that they wish that they never had this orientation. In fact they implicitly wish the taboo had worked in their life. Many are resentful towards God and their family, or towards some institution like the Church. They feel that they are deprived of having a family of their own through no conscious free choice of their own. The annual gay rights parades might leave the thoughtful observer with the impression that they do protest too much to really be delighted with their situation. No one likes to see personally innocent people hurt by a taboo. The fact that many homosexual people and those with other sexual difficulties did not choose to have these problems is often denied by the prejudiced. These fail to accept the individual. They sin as much as those who are tolerant rather than accepting.

Those who wish to pastorally serve Christians struggling with a homosexual identity or tendencies can easily be drawn from acceptance of the individual to tolerance and then to approval without really realizing what is going on. Then, when they are criticized for going against the Christian moral tradition, including the teaching of St. Paul, they will find themselves defending what they once only tolerated. This dangerous progression is observable in many morally controversial areas of life. The helper becomes an enabler, and the enabler turns into a militant. In a time like our own, where objective truth is rarely recognized and even thought about, many thoughtless people will find themselves being vulnerable to this negative progress.

The inescapable fact is that the Christian moral tradition, and even more obviously the teaching of the Catholic Church at this very time in its highest pastoral office, consistently identifies direct homosexual acts as seriously sinful. Many have difficulty with this teaching, not because it is true or traditional, but because it is very challenging to those who wish to be free to do as they please. The crux of the problem is not simply homosexuality. It is the denial of objective truth and moral obligation.

Nurture vs. Nature

But what about the case of the many who did not choose to be homosexual? This is probably the vast majority. The debate over whether a homosexual or even a heterosexual identity is innate or acquired has raged for decades. The assumption — and it is nothing more than an assumption — that if a person is "naturally" homosexually-oriented there is no moral responsibility, has caused many pastoral people to offer explicit or tacit dispensations from the Natural Law and the teaching of the Church. On the other hand, a number of authoritative church documents and guidelines have recommended compassion and understanding of those who experience and struggle with a "homosexual orientation," without ever morally condoning homosexual acts. There is an obvious pressure on bishops to condone what is forbidden even by the New Testament.

The debate on the genetic component of homosexuality itself has tended to be an either/or, black and white sort of affair. The fact is that the whole understanding of the psychological roots of individual personality differences has recently gone through quite a profound revolution. This revolution is largely unrecognized by the general public because of its complexity, and because no one side has come out clearly victorious. (It is too complex for the covers of news magazines.) Until the last decade or two, personality was seen to be entirely either the result of environment or learned behavior or conscious decision (a view more often held by those who had minimal training in psychology.) Only recently, and with much hesitation because of previous abuse by the Nazis and other less virulent racists, there is a focus on the genetic or inherited components of personality. It is dawning on those in the behavioral sciences, and the pastoral people allied with them for religious motives (a large group, myself included), that the roots of personality are at least four-fold, namely: the environment, learning, genetics, and self-determination or free-will. It is worth mentioning in passing that although those who accept the concept of grace may more easily see it operative in self-determination, a little thought will open possibilities of seeing the providential hand of God in all four of these sources.

When this new understanding in the behavioral sciences is adequately grasped, the question of homosexual orientation is seen differently, as are many other aspects of personal identity. The person is much more complex and possibly a much more adaptable creature than any of us thought in the immediate past. Any observer of the passing scene will soon realize that there are many who defy the odds arising from the environment or learning or even genetics. Helen Keller, for instance, beat the genetic odds with a combination of learning, environment and determination — and many of us would say, with help from God's grace. If it is possible to go beyond determining factors like environment, learning and genetics, with self-determination assisted by grace, is it possible for someone to reverse a life-long homosexual orientation or to lead a life of sexual abstinence?

While there are many who, because of their own personal experience of a life of total homosexual attraction, feel that they are simply homosexual, there are others who set out to beat the odds against them. There are a number of people who claim to have successfully gone through a psycho-sexual identity transformation. Frequently these remarkable people include in their readjustment a significant component of prayer and an appeal to God's grace, and they succeed in marrying and raising a family. Others decide that all they can do to is follow the teaching of Scripture and remain simply celibate with a homosexual orientation. These people are often celibate successfully by living an active spiritual life, including good works and generous assistance to others with similar difficulties. Frequently, those homosexually-orientated people who do not find a psycho-sexual transformation possible discover that they need the emotional support of others leading a similar courageous lifestyle. They observe both chastity and modesty, a forgotten virtue that calls one to avoid behavior or situations dangerous to the observance of chastity.

It may come as a surprise to many to know that those who were sexual partners may live chastely together. I myself know a number of people who once lived together in homosexual relationships who now share the same domicile but lead scrupulously chaste lives as friends. It is conceivable that the only way that they were going to lead a chaste life was with the emotional support of another person struggling with the same difficult adjustment. They now have the love of a chaste friendship. Now it is my pastoral impression that such people, having gained chastity, merely need to communicate to their close circle of relatives and friends that they are living a chaste Christian life, in order to avoid misunderstanding and confusing others. I would not have thought this possible but we live and learn.

When someone overcomes genetics or any other factors, most will say that grace is the defining component. St. Augustine's prayer in the face of his own well-known sexual compulsions sums up this experience: "O Lord, command what you will, and permit what you will command." These are the people who find Fr. Harvey and many groups like Courage appealing. Most of these groups are Evangelical-Protestant and share an umbrella group called Exodus. On a spiritual but non-denominational level, there are many successful Twelve-Step programs, especially Sexaholics Anonymous. The pastoral care of souls courageous enough to be chaste and who are often very devout and loving people is a blessing for all who work with them. It should be noted that a number of psychiatrists and psychologists have also made outstanding contributions in this area by working out successful therapeutic programs for the many who seek both spiritual and psychological assistance.

The Pastoral Question

It is a pastor's joy to work with believers serious about their moral and spiritual commitments, sensitive to the inspiration of the Holy Spirit and dedicated to works of charity. It may happen that any serious Christian struggling on the way may fall, but this is what repentance and the sacrament of Reconciliation are about. It is also rewarding to work with those who are moving along the way, but who are not themselves yet there. They have the painful experience of the struggling that Augustine described above. They reach out, but they fall back; and they reach out again. But what about those who want to be a part of the life of the Church but are unwilling, or perhaps at the moment unable to change and give up sinful ways? How is one a pastor and not an enabler? The answer to this question is ... carefully. My suggestions are the following:

1. Be clear in your own mind about the objective moral law taught by the Church and its pastoral consequences. "Blessed are they who walk in the Law of the Lord." But unblessed are they who do not. Many spiritual disasters have occurred ("shipwrecks," St Paul calls them) because confused Christians did not follow this teaching.

2. Always be polite and kind, in a non-condescending way. I call this the Mother Teresa method. I always observed Mother Teresa relate to people whose moral lives were complete disasters, as if she thought they

were making a daily Holy Hour. Many good Christians get themselves tied up in knots here. How do I treat an obviously homosexual person? The answer is ... like everybody else. In social situations, you neither approve nor disapprove. You simply accept the person as he or she is. If they seem to be looking for approval a silent smile will often be the best answer, as Mother Teresa often demonstrated.

3. If anyone asks you what your thinking about this subject is, you must answer honestly and directly, but do not personalize your answer. Be as objective as possible and back off if they insist on your giving them a personal judgement of their behavior. First of all, none of us knows anything about another's responsibility before God. Simply say, "I think homosexual acts are forbidden." Why? Tell them to read something as ancient as St. Paul's Letter to the Romans, or as contemporary as Pope John Paul II's teaching on this issue, and they will see why.

4. Invite and welcome people to all that they can legitimately participate in, as regards the life of the Church. All Catholics are obliged to attend the Liturgy on Sunday and to support the Church in various undertakings.

5. When it comes to the Sacraments, it becomes more difficult, not because the teaching is unclear, but because it is largely unenforced. The norm is quite simple. No one should approach any Sacrament when he/she is in the state of serious sin, except the Sacrament of Reconciliation, and only then when he/she is repentant. On the other hand the norm of the Church is that no one should be refused the Holy Eucharist in public, except a public and notorious sinner (for instance, someone publicly excommunicated). A person leading a homosexual lifestyle, but not militantly opposed to the teachings of the Church, does not qualify as a "public and notorious sinner," any more than a well-known drunk does. This does not mean that their reception of the Eucharist is proper or allowed. It is forbidden, but that is different from saying that it should be publicly refused. In the privacy of the sacrament of Reconciliation, it is a different matter; the sacrament can be refused if the person does not have the purpose of amendment and other proper dispositions.

6. What about the persons who honestly state that their consciences do not burden them? They are living in a relationship with another person of the same sex or of the opposite sex without marriage. They have what is called an erroneous conscience. There is a responsibility to inform a person with an erroneous conscience, although, according to St. Alphonsus Liguori, in his "Practice of a Confessor," there may be

occasions when one does not inform an erroneous conscience because a person will not or can not listen.

This is one of the more subtle pastoral questions. If we do not inform those with erroneous consciences, we sin by omission and even lack of true charity. If we inform them too directly or often, we may drive them away. It seems that a partial answer is to be found in solid preaching about a truly devout and moral life and the necessity of following the New Testament and the Church's teaching. When it comes to individual instruction or even admonition, one should pray fervently to the Holy Spirit to prepare the heart of the individual to receive the message. Christianity is not merely a religious movement. It is a personal relationship of faith and hope in Christ, and all of its questions must be answered on this deeply personal level.

7. We have learned from Alcoholics Anonymous that the best people to assist others in a conversion from compulsive or driven behavior are those recovering from the problem themselves. Courage has proven this again. The best person to lead a homosexual person to a chaste life is a chaste homosexual follower of Christ. The truth of this is brought out by the many who are growing in what Alcoholics Anonymous calls the Twelfth Step. Also, the danger of tolerance is highlighted by the persistent oppositions of those who resist moral conversion on the part of those unwilling to accept the Church's teaching. The almost unbelievable fact that there are Catholics opposed to Courage and similar authentic movements demonstrates the depth of moral confusion and relativism that passes for pastoral concern.

This brings up the oxymoron of "gay-lesbian ministry." Truth be told, there simply is no such Christian ministry, any more than there is a ministry to "drunks." There is a very needed ministry to homosexual persons and recovering alcoholics. The terms "gay and lesbian" mean the acceptance of a lifestyle with a commitment to immoral behavior. Homosexual is a condition; gay and lesbian is a decision, a commitment which is powerfully denounced by St. Paul. It is my personal conviction that the accepted use of these terms for a ministry is a profound cause of confusion for the faithful and a dangerous spiritual disservice to those who have a right to be shepherded by the Church.

A Final Word

Christ came to save sinners. And we all are sinners. We all need to acknowledge our sins and make progress every day. This can only be done by prayer and being led by the teaching of Christ and his Church. Christ calls us all to chastity in our own vocation. This call is addressed to all, both the married and the single. We need to keep in mind that when we do not call others to following the way of Christ, we endanger their salvation and our own. Prayer, self-knowledge and the obedience of faith are the true guides to any attempt to shepherd souls on behalf of the Good Shepherd of us all.

Chapter Seven

Biomedical Research with "Decisionally Incapacitated" Human Subjects:

Legalization of a Defunct Normative Bioethics Theory

Dr. DIANE N. IRVING [1]

Consider this scenario: Martha is legally defined as a "decisionally incapacitated" person. That is, she is at least eighteen years of age and cannot give a valid, informed consent for research participation because she cannot sufficiently understand the nature, extent, or probable

---

[1] Only a very few people we encounter leave a really positive, profound and enduring imprint and influence on our lives. As retreat master in my high school, my professor of moral theology in college, founder and president of the De Sales School of Theology where I taught philosophy for nine years, family friend, minister of my son's marriage, and advisor to me on an endless number of issues over the years, Fr. John Harvey has had such an influence on me and my work. This essay is humbly and lovingly dedicated to him in celebration of his remarkable life and works, and in deep gratitude for the glorious and amazingly integrated gifts of priest, scholar, pastor and friend he has so generously shared with me and millions of others. His dauntless courage, boundless enthusiasm, incorrigible search for and defense of truth, and deep gentle love for God, His people and His Church are truly unique, and shine endlessly as an example and source of strength and joy for us all. Thank you, Fr. John.

consequences of the proposed research participation, cannot make a sufficient evaluation of its burdens, risks, and benefits, or cannot communicate a decision. However, she has also been determined to be "competent" by the same psychiatric researcher into whose scientific protocol she would be enrolled, and able to give informed consent to sign an Advanced Directive for Research Participation. Martha can also choose a Research Agent who would then use his/her "substituted judgment" that Martha would have wanted to participate in high risk, no direct benefit, "research-in-general" for the benefit of future possible groups or "classes" of persons with the same or similar diseases or conditions, for the advancement of scientific knowledge, or for obtaining information which could not be obtained in any other way - were she competent. Other consenters - health care agents, surrogates, and "monitors" appointed by the IRB - could also enroll Martha in other categories of research protocols, including "emergency room research." There would be no civil or criminal liability to physicians, researchers, consenters, or IRB members for any harms or injuries sustained by Martha during her participation in the research, nor any compensation for harms or injuries, or follow-up medical care. And unknown to her "normal, healthy" neighbors, all Advanced Directives for Standard Medical Care and Treatment could be convertible to Advanced Directives for Research Participation like Martha's, enabling consenters for standard medical care to enroll them in similar therapeutic and non-therapeutic research protocols if and when they should become "decisionally incapacitated."

Such would actually be the case if the proposed statute[2] in the State of Maryland addressing biomedical research involving "decisionally incapacitated" persons were to pass the Maryland legislature. The rationale (OD, 37) for such provisions are clearly stated in the October 1996 draft by the Working Group under Jack Schwartz, the Assistant Attorney General (although not repeated in following drafts). In that draft, their interpretation of the bioethics principles of autonomy, justice, and beneficence (or what is known as "principalism" or the "Georgetown Mantra"), as articulated in the Belmont Report[3], and which ground the federal OPRR regulations and Common Rule[4] for research involving human subjects, are cited and accepted *per se* as the grounding of this Maryland State proposed statute. However, I would argue that the interpretation of these bioethics principles by the Working Group seems quite unbalanced. Their interpretation of "beneficence" leans very heavily towards utility, "autonomy" seems to be taken to an extreme, and "justice" is almost obliterated. The Working Group seems to be oblivious that the bioethics principles have had multiple and often contentious

---

[2] Office of the Maryland Attorney General, J. Joseph Curran, Jr., Attorney General, Jack Schwartz, Assistant Attorney General, INITIAL REPORT OF THE ATTORNEY GENERAL'S RESEARCH WORKING GROUP (October 1996 draft, hereinafter referred to in text as OD); with Schwartz's Letter (hereinafter referred to in text as OD/S), and May 1997 draft (hereinafter referred to in text as MD). It is noted that almost all of the research in this proposed statute has recently been rejected as unconstitutional by the New York Supreme Court, Appellate Division (*see* T.D. v. The New York State Office of Mental Health, 1996 WL 695417 (N.Y.A.D. 1/Dept.). See also Philip J. Hilts, *New York Court strikes down rules for psychiatric studies of children and mentally ill*, THE NEW YORK TIMES, Dec. 27, 1996, at A1; Frank J. Ayd, M.D. (ed.), *"Decisionally incapacitated" persons and a proposed Maryland statute*, 35 THE MEDICAL-MORAL NEWSLETTER 3/4, 9-16 (1998).
[3] The National Commission for the Protection of Human Subjects of Biomedical and Behavioral Research, U.S. Department of Health, Education and Welfare, THE BELMONT REPORT: ETHICAL PRINCIPLES AND GUIDELINES FOR THE PROTECTION OF HUMAN SUBJECTS OF RESEARCH (1978) (hereinafter THE BELMONT REPORT).
[4] U.S. Code of Federal Regulations, Title 45 Public Welfare, Part 46 - Dept. of Health and Human Services - PROTECTION OF HUMAN SUBJECTS (1991) (hereinafter noted as OPRR REGULATIONS).

interpretations even from their inception,[5] that bioethics principalism is a *normative* ethical theory (i.e., it takes a stand on what is right or wrong),[6] that there is no such thing as a "neutral ethics" for public policy or law,[7] or that bioethics principalism has been declared inoperative and unworkable by even those leaders in bioethics who helped to create and foster it so many years.[8]

Regardless of one's interpretation of these bioethics principles, and aside from the very strong possibility of serious concrete harm to multitudes of "decisionally incapacitated" human subjects as a result of certain interpretations, the adoption of this proposed statute would, in effect, result in the *legalization* of a very normative *non-neutral* theory of ethics which would be imposed on all citizens of the State of Maryland (and other states, if this were to set a legal precedent). This goal is

---

[5] THE BELMONT REPORT, *supra* note 2. There exists an extensive literature on this issue. Compare the Belmont Report's treatment of autonomy with that of: PRINCIPLES OF BIOMEDICAL ETHICS (Thomas L. Beauchamp & James Childress, 1979), at 60, 135, 169; and CONTEMPORARY ISSUES IN BIOETHICS (Thomas L. Beauchamp & LeRoy Walters eds., 1982), at 23-39. *See also* PRINCIPLES OF HEALTH CARE ETHICS (Ranaan Gillon ed., 1994)(which contains dozens of articles and debates, especially in Part I); and many of the articles *infra*.

[6] *See* Beauchamp & Childress, *supra* note 4, at 7-9; Beauchamp & Walters, *supra* note 4, at 1-3.

[7] *See* Dianne N. Irving, *Which ethics for science and public policy?*, 3 ACCT. IN RES. 77, 77-100 (1993); D. Irving, *Academic fraud and conceptual transfer in bioethics: Abortion, human embryo research and psychiatric research*, in LIFE AND LEARNING: PROCEEDINGS OF THE FOURTH UNIVERSITY FACULTY FOR LIFE CONFERENCE, JUNE 1994 (Joseph W. Koterski, ed., 1995), at 193-215; D. Irving, *Quality assurance auditors: Between a rock and a hard place*, 3 QUALITY ASSURANCE: GOOD PRACTICE, REGULATION, AND LAW 1, 33-52 (1994); and many of the articles *infra*.

[8] Daniel Callahan, *Bioethics: private choice and common ground*, HASTINGS CENTER REP. May-June 1994, at 31; Albert Jonsen, *Preface*, in WHAT ABOUT PRINCIPLES: FERMENT IN U.S. BIOETHICS (DuBose et al., eds., 1994); see also Ranaan Gillon, *supra* note 4; Amy Gutmann and Dennis Thompson, *Deliberating about bioethics*, HASTINGS CENTER REP. May-June 1997, at 38-41; Leonard S. Rubenstein, *Standards of accountability for consent in research*, in ETHICS IN NEUROBIOLOGICAL RESEARCH WITH HUMAN SUBJECTS: THE BALTIMORE CONFERENCE ON ETHICS (Adil E. Shamoo, ed., 1997), at 129-138.

actually articulated in the October 1996 draft: "The goal of this project is that '[f]or a change, law may be the handmaiden of ethics and ethics served by the law rather than vice versa'" (OD, 3).

The "ethics" they opt for is "secular" bioethics principalism. (It is unfortunate that the on-going drafts do not continue to provide this rationale for the citizens of Maryland.) However, the larger question which needs to be addressed is: should bioethics principalism be enshrined into local, state or federal law, especially now that it is summarily a non-operative normative ethical theory?

Nevertheless, in this limited article the pros and cons of the validity of bioethics, or of its legalization, will not be fully addressed. The focus, instead, will be simply to identify and briefly comment on a short list of ethical and legal concerns associated with this proposed statute which do flow directly from these questionable (and unchallenged) premises of the Working Group.

Short List of Concerns

The following is merely a very short list of some of the major legal and ethical concerns presented in this proposed legal statute as expressed in the October 1996 and the May 1997 drafts:

Equating standard medical care with therapeutic research

One of the major concerns with this proposed statute, and one from which much of the other concerns below flow, is its unique equation of "standard medical care or treatment" with "therapeutic research":

> If particular research has the potential for direct medical benefit to the individual, as determined by the institutional review board, and therefore could be considered a type of "health care," then the HCDA [Health Care Decisions Act] applies to participation in the research protocol as if the research were a treatment option like any other. If, however, a research protocol has no potential for direct medical benefit, the HCDA does not address the matter. [OD, 2] (insert mine)

Along the same lines, and included in the back of the October draft is a letter by Jack Schwartz to the Working Group to further clarify this equation:

The term 'health care' [as used in the HCDA] is not defined. However, other provisions in the Act make its meaning clear. It is synonymous with a procedure or course of treatment that relates to the disease state of the particular patient. ... This decisional framework, requiring a "health care" judgment in terms of the patient's assumed decision about a treatment, works well enough for therapeutic research. So long as there is an articulable link between the research and a possible improvement in the patient's condition, then a "health care" decision is possible, and the patient's hypothesized wishes would be the basis for it. [OD/S, 2]

Thus the logic of the proposed statute seems to go like this: If a treatment or procedure is "medically beneficial," then it is a form of "health care." Both standard medical care and therapeutic research can possibly be "medically beneficial." Therefore both standard medical care and therapeutic research are forms of "health care." In effect, this equates standard medical care with therapeutic research for purposes of this proposed statute.

That is why in the proposed statute a "health care agent," or any substitute, who is allowed to make standard medical "health care" decisions for an incompetent person, can also make "health care" decisions concerning the person's participation in therapeutic research. That is also why, when a health care agent, or other consenter, makes decisions about "medical best interests" for a person, those "medical best interests" can include possible medical benefits from participating in therapeutic research. This, in effect, also makes an Advanced Directive for standard medical care equivalent to an Advanced Directive for Research Participation (the on-going interpretation in a policy for the "cognitively impaired" at NIH since 1985),[9] and both can be used to enroll "decisionally incapacitated" persons in non-therapeutic research for groups or a "class," or in non-therapeutic research for the advancement of scientific knowledge or to obtain information which cannot be obtained otherwise, etc.

---

[9] John Fletcher, E. Dommel & D. Cowell, *A trial policy for the intramural programs of the National Institutes of Health: consent to research with impaired human subjects*, 7 IRB 1985, at 1-6; Philip Candilis et al., *A survey of researchers using a consent policy for cognitively impaired human research subjects*, 15 IRB 1993, at 1-4; Trey Suderland & Ruth Dukoff, *Informed consent with cognitively impaired patients: an NIMH perspective of the durable power of attorney*, 4 ACCT. IN RES. 217, 217-226 (1996).

Although the Belmont Report is needlessly vague on the fundamental distinction between standard medical care and research,[10] and on other key related points as well, most international codes of medical research ethics, adopted by the United States government, have always articulated a real distinction between standard medical care/treatment and research. For example, the Declaration of Helsinki (1964, 1975, 1983, 1989)[11] divides these activities into three basic categories: (1) standard medical care or treatment; and (2) research, which itself is further divided into (2a) medical research combined with clinical care (clinical research), usually referred to as "therapeutic research" and (2b) non-clinical biomedical research, usually referred to as non-therapeutic research. These distinctive kinds of activities are distinguished primarily according to their different aims, goals, or purposes and according to whether or not there is direct medical benefit to a particular patient or not. With reference to defining "research," the Declaration states:

> The purpose of biomedical research involving human subjects must be to improve diagnostic, therapeutic and prophylactic procedures and the understanding of the aetiology and pathogenesis of disease... In the field of biomedical research a fundamental distinction must be recognized between medical research in which the aim is essentially diagnostic or therapeutic for a patient, and medical research, the essential object of which is purely scientific and without implying direct diagnostic or therapeutic value to the person subjected to the research. [Intro.] ... The physician can combine medical research with professional care, the object being the acquisition of new medical knowledge, only to the extent the medical research is justified by its potential diagnostic or therapeutic value

---

[10] *See* THE BELMONT REPORT, *supra* note 2, at 3.

[11] *Declaration of Helsinki*, in United States Department of Health and Human Services, OFFICE FOR THE PROTECTION OF RESEARCH RISKS: 1993, PROTECTING HUMAN RESEARCH SUBJECTS: INSTITUTIONAL REVIEW BOARD GUIDEBOOK (1993), at A6-3 to A6-6. See also, *Nuremburg Code*, at A6-1 to A6-2; United Nations (1947) *Universal Declaration of Human Rights*; United Nations (1991) *Principles for the Protection of Persons with Mental Illness and for the Improvement of Mental Health Care*; and *International Covenant on Civil and Political Rights* (ratified, Sen. Comm. on Foreign Affairs 1992). For a review, see Eric Rosenthal, *The International Covenant on Civil and Political Rights and the rights of research subjects*, in Shamoo (ed.), *supra* note 7, at 265-272.

for the patient. [Medical research combined with clinical care - clinical research][12] (inserts mine)

Note that in the first kind of research (i.e., "clinical research") the goals of performing biomedical research to improve diagnostic, therapeutic and prophylactic procedures and the understanding of the aetiology and pathogenesis of disease are referred to as *research*, not as standard medical care or "health care"; and the possible benefits must accrue to the *individual patient* and not to "others." Both of these elements are changed in the proposed Maryland statute. The second category of research is clearly defined as "non-therapeutic biomedical research" or "non-clinical biomedical research," where the research would not be for the direct benefit of a particular patient but rather for the advancement of scientific knowledge, to obtain information that cannot be obtained in any other way, etc.

It is this blurring of the fundamental distinction between "standard medical care" and "therapeutic research" which is used to justify much of what follows.

Redefining categories of research

In the May 1997 draft of this proposed statute, even new and different categories of "research" are used: "expected benefit research" and "no expected benefit research" (MD, 10-15). "Expected benefit research" now explicitly includes research which, essentially, investigates diagnostic, therapeutic, and prophylactic procedures and the understanding of the aetiology and pathogenesis of diseases, but which can be beneficial *only* to a group or "class" of possible future persons with the same or similar diseases or conditions. However, research performed for these purposes and for a group or a "class" is unequivocally non-therapeutic research, since there is no direct medical benefit to a particular individual patient. The category of "no expected benefit" research in the May 1997 draft essentially retains the traditional meaning of non-therapeutic research.

Nevertheless, "expected benefit research" now includes, by definition, "non-therapeutic research" for a group or a "class" instead of only for a particular person. The two categories of therapeutic and non-therapeutic

---

[12] *Declaration of Helsinki, supra* note 10, at A6-3 to A6-9.

research are commingled and confused, and both are redefined under "expected benefit" research.

The logic of the proposed statute seems to go something like this: Research that is "medically beneficial" is therapeutic research. Research for a group or "class" of possible future persons with the same or similar diseases or conditions is "medically beneficial." Therefore, research for a group or a "class" is therapeutic research (which has already been equated with "health care"). The critical phrase, *"beneficial only to a particular patient,"* has been left out of the equation.

If some are confused as to where to draw the line between benefits to a particular individual and benefits to groups, "classes," or society, etc., the Declaration of Helsinki and other codes offer clear guidance:

> Concern for the interests of the subject must always prevail over the interests of science and society. [Basic principles] ... The physician can combine medical research with professional care, the objective being the acquisition of new medical knowledge, only to the extent that medical research is justified by its potential diagnostic or therapeutic value for the patient. [Medical research combined with clinical care - clinical research] ... In research on man, the interests of science and society should never take precedence over considerations related to the wellbeing of the subject. [Non-therapeutic biomedical research involving human subjects - non-clinical biomedical research][13] (inserts mine)

Redefining risk categories

Risk categories have never been successfully defined, including those offered in the Belmont Report or in the OPRR regulations. The bioethics literature[14] does contain numerous works which at least attempt to

---

[13] *Declaration of Helsinki, supra* note 10, at A6-4 to A6-6.

[14] See generally early works by A.S. Tannenbaum & R.A. Cook, *Report on the Mentally Infirm*, in RESEARCH INVOLVING THOSE INSTITUTIONALIZED AS MENTALLY INFIRM: APPENDIX (National Commission for the Protection of Human Subjects of Biomedical and Behavioral Research, 1978), at 1-2; Bernard Barber, INFORMED CONSENT IN MEDICAL THERAPY AND RESEARCH (1978), at 10-13. For more current works, *see* Rubenstein, *supra* note 7; an excellent legal analysis by Robert A. Destro, *Government oversight*, in Shamoo (ed.), *supra* note 7, at 81-99; Jessica Wilen Berg, *Legal and ethical complexities of consent with cognitively impaired*

articulate three basic categories for purposes of calculating a valid risk/benefit ratio: minimal risk, more than minor risk (or slight increase over minimal risk), and high risk. Obviously human subjects and their consenters are going to want to know what they are getting themselves into.

In both the October and May drafts, it is not made clear that "greater than minimal risk" (OD, p. 7-15) or "more than minor increase over minimal risk" (MD, p. 12-16) includes "high risk" research. However, at least in the October draft these vague risk categories are applied to both "direct benefit research" and to "no direct benefit research." In the May draft, however, there are *no categories of risk* articulated for "expected benefit research"; the risk categories are used only in reference to "no expected benefit" research. This, too, is unprecedented. Both the lack of attempting to articulate a comparable "high risk" category and the total lack of any risk categories for "expected benefit research" in the May draft would make it difficult for any one to know or understand what they were getting into and, therefore, to give a valid informed consent.

However, codes such as the Nuremburg Code, the Declaration of Helsinki, and others, consistently confirm the need for accurate and sound estimates of research risks:

> Every biomedical research project involving human subjects should be preceded by careful assessment of predictable risks in comparison with foreseeable benefits to the subject or to others. Concern for the interests of the subject must always prevail over the interests of science and society. [Basic principles] ... Physicians should abstain from engaging in research projects involving human subjects unless they are satisfied that the hazards involved are believed to be predictable. Physicians should cease any investigation if the hazards are found to outweigh the potential benefits. [Basic principles] ... In any research on human beings, each potential subject must be adequately informed of the aims, methods, anticipated

---

research subjects: proposed guidelines, 24 J.L. MED. & ETHICS 18, 18-35 (1996). Although the OPRR Regulations define "minimal risk" as that in which "the probability and magnitude of harm or discomfort anticipated in the research are not greater in and of themselves than those ordinarily encountered in daily life or during the performance of routine physical or psychological examinations or tests" (section 46.102 [i]), it is questionable whether this definition could realistically refer to all competent adults, much less to children or to persons who are mentally ill or otherwise incapacitated.

benefits and potential hazards of the study and the discomfort it may entail. [Basic principles] .... The potential benefits, hazards and discomfort of a new method should be weighed against the advantages of the best current diagnostic and therapeutic methods. [Clinical research][15] (inserts mine)

Obviously, an accurate determination of risks is critical for purposes of protocol designs, informed consents, and "substituted judgments," as well as knowing when to remove patients from protocols, or determining whether patients should remain on standard treatments. Nevertheless, the May draft would allow a "decisionally incapacitated" person to participate in "expected benefit research" and "no expected benefit research" without it being clear to the researcher, the IRB, "decisionally impaired" patients, or their consenters that high risk research is involved. Informed consent or "substituted judgments" are essentially precluded.

Informed consent by "decisionally impaired" human subjects

The issues as to whether "decisionally incapacitated," "decisionally impaired," "cognitively impaired," or any other "incompetent" persons are truly capable of giving valid informed consents to participate in research protocols, sign any kind of Advanced Directives, or appoint

---

[15] *Declaration of Helsinki, supra* note 10, at A6-4 to A6-5. See also Robert F. Weir & Jay R. Horton, *Genetic research, adolescents, and informed consent,* THEOR. MED. Dec. 1995, at 347-373; Walter Robinson, Commentary, *Family dynamics and children in medical research,* J. CLIN. ETHICS, Winter 1996, at 362-364; Adil E. Shamoo & Dianne N. Irving, *Accountability in research using persons with mental illness,* 3 ACCT. IN RES. 1, 1-17 (1993); A. Shamoo and D. Irving, *A review of patient outcome in pharmacologic studies from the psychiatric literature, 1966-1993,* 3 J. SCIENCE AND ENGINEERING ETH. 4, at 395-405 (1997); *Uninformed patients used as guinea pig,* THE WASHINGTON TIMES, Dec. 16, 1996, at A8; Vera Hassner Sharav, *Independent family advocates challenge the fraternity of silence,* in Shamoo (ed.), *supra* note 7; Janice Becker, *Expanding on a mother's testimony,* in Shamoo (ed.), *supra* note 7; Robert Aller and Gregory Aller, *An institutional response to patient/family/complaints,* in Shamoo (ed.), *supra* note 7, at 155-172; K.J. Rothman & K.B. Michels, *Sounding board - the continuing unethical use of placebo controls,* in Shamoo (ed.), *supra* note 7, at 289-297; but see Robert Temple, *Problems in interpreting active control equivalence trials,* in Shamoo (ed.), *supra* note 7, at 279-287.

consent agents of any sort are still controversial.[16] Theories abound; but solid studies or consensus do not. In fact, the literature contains a great number of arguments to the contrary.

Even the definition of a "decisionally incapacitated individual" in the May draft would seem to preclude any participation of these persons in any of the proposed categories of research:

> "Decisionally incapacitated individual" means an individual who is at least 18 years of age and who *cannot give a valid informed consent for research participation* because the individual cannot sufficiently understand the nature, extent, or probable consequences of the proposed research participation, cannot make a sufficient evaluation of burdens, risks, and benefits of the proposed research participation, or cannot communicate a decision." [MD, 2] (emphasis mine).

Informed consent determined by the psychiatric researcher

"Decisionally incapacitated" patients are to be judged "competent" by the same psychiatric researchers in whose research projects they will participate. This could reasonably be considered the source of a clear conflict of interests. There is also the possibility of more subtle pressures on "decisionally incapacitated" human subjects when the researchers are

---

[16] *See* Rubenstein, *supra* note 7; Berg *supra* note 13; Weir *supra* note 14. See also Paul S. Appelbaum, *Patient's competence to consent to neurobiological research*, 4 ACCT. IN RES. 241, 241-251 (1996); Jesse A Goldner, *An overview of legal controls on human experimentation and the regulatory implications of taking Professor Katz seriously, in Health Law Symposium.* Legal and Ethical Controls on Biomedical Research: Seeking Consent, Avoiding Condescension, 38 ST. LOUIS L.J. 3, 63 (1993); Dianne N. Irving, *Psychiatric research: reality check*, J. CAMI, Spring 1994, at 42-44; Adil E. Shamoo & Dianne N. Irving, *The PSDA and the depressed elderly: "intermittent competency" revisited*, J. CLIN. ETHICS, Spring 1993, at 74-80; Lisa Anne Hawkins, *Living-will statutes: a minor oversight*, 78 VA. L.REV., 1581, 1581-1615 (1992); K.C. Glass and M.A. Somerville, *Informed consent to medical research on persons with Alzheimer's disease: ethical and legal parameters, in* ALZHEIMER'S DISEASE RESEARCH: ETHICAL AND LEGAL ISSUES (Berg et al., (eds.), 1991), at 30-59; H. Helmchen, *The problem of informed consent in dementia research*, 9 MED AND LAW 1206, 1206-1213 (1990).

also the subjects' own psychiatric physicians. This concern is articulated in one of the codes:

> When obtaining informed consent for the research project the physician should be particularly cautious if the subject is in a dependent relationship to him or her or may consent under duress. In that case the informed consent should be obtained by a physician who is not engaged in the investigation and who is completely independent of this official relationship. [Basic principles][17] (insert mine)

But if "decisionally incapacitated" persons are really competent to give informed consent, as testified to by the psychiatric researchers, then why is there any need for all those consenters to begin with? Why can a "competent decisionally incapacitated" person not simply give his/her own informed consent to take part in these research protocols?

Informed consent for "research-in-general"

At least in the October draft there is reference to participation in "a particular" future research protocol. However, the May draft refers only to future unspecified "research" protocols or, what one might term, future "research-in-general." Informed consent would essentially be precluded if human subjects, or their consenters, are not given the specifics of a research protocol in which they would consider participating.

"Substituted judgments"

"Decisionally impaired" competent human subjects will also be able to give informed consent to choose "research agents" who would then give their own "substituted judgments" that the patients would have wanted to participate in research-in-general had they been competent to consent. If the "research agent" is not available to consent, then a "health care agent," a "surrogate," or a "monitor" appointed by the Institutional Review Board (IRB) of the institution can then consent (another possible conflict of interests). Depending on the level of

---

[17] *Declaration of Helsinki, supra* note 10, at A6-5; see also, Dianne N. Irving, *Psychiatric research; Reality check*, 5 J. CALIFORNIA ALLIANCE FOR THE MENTALLY ILL, 1, at 42-44 (1994).

"consent agent," this could include high risk, no direct benefit research for groups or "classes" of possible future persons who might have this or similar diseases or conditions, or even for no direct benefit non-therapeutic research with utilitarian goals such as the advancement of scientific knowledge, the greater social good, national security, or because there is no other way by which scientists can obtain the information. The issue of the use of "substituted judgments" within the context of even Advanced Directives for Standard Medical Care is still very controversial and has been specifically rejected by many courts.[18]

---

[18] See Mathy Mezey et al., *Life-sustaining treatment decisions by spouses of patients with Alzheimer's disease*, J. AM. GERIATRICS SOC., Feb. 1996, at 144-150; David C. Thomasma, *A communal model for presumed consent for research on the neurologically vulnerable*, 4 ACCT. IN RES. 227, 227-239 (1996); Ralph Baergen, *Revisiting the substituted judgment standard*, J. CLIN. ETHICS, Spring 1995, at 30-38; Rosalind E. Ladd & Edwin N. Forman, *Adolescent decision-making: giving weight to age-specific values*, THEOR. MED., Dec. 1995, at 333-345; Jeremiah Suhl et al., *Myth of substituted judgment: surrogate decision-making regarding life support is unreliable*, 154 ARCHIVES OF INTERNAL MED., 90, 90-96 (1994); John Hardwig, *The problem of proxies with interests of their own: toward a better theory of proxy decisions*, J. CLIN. ETH. Spring 1993, at 20-27; James Coyne King, *The search for objectivity in applying the substituted judgment rule in medical care cases*, 37 BOSTON BAR JOURNAL 10, 10-12, 14 (1993); Robert A. Perlman et al., *Contributions of empirical research to medical ethics*, THEOR. MED, Sept. 1993, at 197-210; Lynne E. Lebit, *Compelled medical procedures involving minors and incompetents and misapplication of the substituted judgment doctrine*, J. OF LAW AND HEALTH (1992-1993), at 107-130; Alexander M. Capron, *Substituting our judgment*, HASTINGS CENTER REP. March-April 1992, at 58-59; Ezekiel J. Emanuel & Linda L. E. Emanuel, *Proxy decision-making for incompetent patients: an ethical and empirical analysis*, 267 JAMA, 2067, 2067-2071 (1992); Jan Hare et al, *Agreement between patients and their self-selected surrogates on difficult medical decisions*, 152 ARCHIVES OF INTERNAL MED., 1049, 1049-1054 (1992); Thomas G. Gulkeil & Paul S. Appelbaum, *Substituted judgment: best interests in disguise*, HASTING CENTER REPORT, June 1983, at 8-11. For court decisions, see Illinois. Appelate Court, First District, Fourth Division. In re C.A. North Eastern Reporter, 2nd series. 1992 Oct 15 (date of decision). 603:1171-1194; Illinois. Supreme Court. Curran v. Bosze. North Eastern Reporter, 2nd series. 1990 Dec. 20 (date of decision). 566:1319-1345; Florida. District Court of Appeal, Second District. In re Guardianship of Browing. Southern Reporter, 2nd series.

Distortion of the principle of "autonomy"

Allowing "decisionally incapacitated" patients to give informed consent is done under the pretext of "respecting the 'decisionally incapacitated' patient's autonomy." In the May draft this includes the patient's participation in high-risk non-therapeutic research which would have no direct benefit to the individual patient. Such an interpretation of "autonomy" is a distortion of that bioethics principle, now being redefined and applied as an absolute right regardless of anything and without limitations. This was hardly the Belmont Report's original meaning of the bioethics principle of "autonomy," which was first referred to as "respect for persons" — a term which then included both autonomous and non-autonomous persons (who, according to this principle, are respected *by protecting them from harm*),[19] and which initially was neither understood nor presented as an absolute bioethics principle. In fact, the bioethics principles were declared to be "*prima facie*," i.e., no single principle could out-weigh any other principle.[20] Of course, the problem then became how to resolve conflicts among the principles, conflicts which bioethics theory itself never could resolve — a major reason for the internal collapse of bioethics principalism.

This distortion of the principle of "autonomy" would allow for considerable potential abuses of "decisionally incapacitated" patients. "Respecting" a patient's supposed "absolute autonomy" is understandably appealing to those who advocate for the "decisionally disabled" and to others who want to preserve their "rights." But in reality, it could obviously lead directly to great physical and psychological harm and

---

1989 Apr. 10 (date of decision). 543:258-276; Missouri. Supreme Court, en banc. Cruzan by Cruzan v. Harmon. South Western Reporter, 2nd Series. 1988 Nov 16 (date of decision). 760:408-445. *See also*, George J. Annas, *Precatory and mindless mimicry: the case of Mary O'Connor*, HASTINGS CENTER REP., Dec. 1988, at. 31-33.

[19] See THE BELMONT REPORT, *supra* note 10, at 4. See also James F. Childress, *The place of autonomy in bioethics*, HASTINGS CENTER REP. Jan./Feb. 1990, at 12-17; PROTECTING THE VULNERABLE: AUTONOMY AND CONSENT IN HEALTH CARE (Margret Brazier and Mary Lobjoit, 1991).

[20] See Beauchamp & Childress, *supra* note 4, at 45-47; Beauchamp & Walters, *supra* note 4, at 23, 35-36.

injury precisely to those same vulnerable patients in areas in which they should actually be protected from abuse.

IRB incompetence

The reality of "unchecked research" and of the ineffectiveness of an IRB to competently review the research and/or to protect the patients from harm and abuse has historically been demonstrated to be problematic, and is under serious scrutiny now by both Rep. Shays and Sen. Glen,[21] who are conducting hearings on this and related research issues. If an IRB does not work, or is so compromised by bias and incompetence, then what justifies its continuing use in any research using any human subjects? Two interesting new phenomena concerning the IRB are: "IRB shopping," where drug or device companies go to a different IRB until they find one which will not reject their research protocols, and "deferred consent," where incompetent patients are enrolled in research

---

[21] *Health and Human Services Oversight Hearings on Bioethics, May 8, 1997.* See Sheryl Gay Stolberg, *"Unchecked" experiments on people raise concern*, THE NEW YORK TIMES, May 14, 1997, at A1. In that article, Gary Ellis states, "There is unchecked human experimentation taking place. ... My estimate is that there is a substantial reservoir of research activity that occurs beyond the boundary of existing rules and policies" (at A16). In that same article Art Caplan comments on one of the problems with the existing Institutional Review Board regulations under the present Common Rule: "The old model presumes that you would do research to find out some important new basic facts about health. ... Current research might be for a pharmaceutical company to put a new drug on the market to compete with the five ones that are already there for, say, insomnia or weight loss. The risks and benefits may be different," (at A16). For this and other problems with existing federal Institutional Review Boards, see generally Jay Katz, *Human experimentation and human rights*, 38 ST. LOUIS UNIV. LAW REV., 7, 7 (1993); Goldner, *supra* note 15; J. Thomas Puglisi & Gary B. Ellis, *Neurobiological research involving human subjects: perspective from the Office for the Protection from Research Risks*, in Shamoo (ed.), *supra* note 7, at 273-277; Sue Hoppe, *Institutional Review Boards and research on individuals with mental disorders*, in Shamoo (ed.), *supra* note 7, at 101-109; Robert A. Destro, *supra* note 13, at 81-99; Robert J. Levine, *Proposed regulations for research involving those institutionalized as mentally infirm: a consideration of their relevance in 1995*, in Shamoo (ed.), *supra* note 7, at 45-54; Frederick J. Frese, *A consumer/professional's view of ethics in research*, in Shamoo (ed.), *supra* note 7, at 191-194.

protocols without their informed consent, and only later, after the fact, their informed consent (or proxy consent by a surrogate) is obtained.[22]

Appendix B

In the back of the May 1997 draft, Appendix B would appear only to increase the list of surrogate consenters in an Advanced Directive for Standard Medical Care in the present Maryland Health Care Decisions Act. They could then consent for standard medical treatment for a once-competent patient who later becomes incompetent if none of the other consenters is available. This list includes spouses, siblings, adult children, other relatives, friends, etc. However, if the new proposed statute becomes law, these additional surrogate consenters for standard medical care could also consent to enroll any patient — "decisionally incapacitated" or otherwise — in medical research protocols, since the new proposed statute, in essence, would allow Advanced Directives for Standard Medical Care to be convertible with Advanced Directives for Research Participation.

---

[22] On "IRB shopping," see Stolberg, *supra* note 20. In that article, Rep. Shays is represented as being "startled by the testimony, including accounts of ethics panels - called institutional review boards, or I.R.B.'s - set up as profit-making ventures to evaluate proposed experiments for research groups that pay them." Rep. Shays states: "I am struck by the fact that we have I.R.B.'s that can be created by anyone, that we don't even know how many there are. I think the more we get into this the more we are going to realize how casual this process really is" (at A1). In the same article, Art Caplan is represented as commenting on "the boom in research paid for by private industry [that] has created a new phenomenon: commercial review boards that have generated a wave of what Dr. Caplan called 'I.R.B. shopping' by researchers" (A16). On "deferred consent," see generally Robert J. Levine, *Research in emergency situations: the role of deferred consent*, Editorial, 273 JAMA 1300, 1300-1302 (1995); Robert J. Levine, *Deferred consent*, 12 CONTROL CLIN. TRIALS, 546, 546-550 (1991); Michelle H. Biros et al., *Informed consent in emergency research: consensus statement from the coalition conference of acute resuscitation and critical care researchers*, 273 JAMA 1283, 1283-1287, (1995); Kenneth V. Iserson & Douglas Lindsey, *Research on critically ill and injured patients: rules, reality, and ethics*, 13 J. OF EMERG. MED. 563,563-567 (1995); J.H.T. Karlawish & G. A. Sachs, *Research on the cognitively impaired: lessons and warnings from the emergency research debate*, 45 J. AM. GERIATR. SOC. 474-481.

Distortion of the principle of "beneficence"

Given that one could find in the Belmont Report justification for defining "beneficence" as including benefits to society, etc., as well as to individuals,[23] the Working Group seems to lean quite heavily on a purely utilitarian interpretation of it. For example, under "expected benefit research" in the May draft, the "benefit" part of the risk/benefit ratio can refer *only* to benefits to a group or "class," rather than referring *only* to a particular individual patient. As the May draft states:

> **Expected benefit research**: (a) This section applies to research that: (1) presents a reasonable prospect of direct medical benefit to the class of decisionally incapacitated individuals who have been authorized by an IRB to be enrolled in the research; **or** (2) pertains to a disorder or condition of a decisionally incapacitated individual and presents a reasonable prospect of direct medical benefit to that individual. (MD, 10) (emphasis mine)

When a consenter is to consider "medical *best* interests," this beneficence could also refer only to "society," for the advancement of scientific knowledge, etc. The inclusion of purely non-therapeutic no direct benefit research in this proposed statute can be justified as "medical benefits" and considered as "best medical interests" to society:

> But suppose there is no scientific evidence that participation is reasonably likely to offer benefits to the patient. The Act's "best interest" calculus does not include potential benefits to society as a whole, or even to those who might suffer from the same disease in the future. Participation in research of that kind, even with minimal risk, is not a "health care" decision within the meaning of the Act. ... If ultimately we think that health care agents or surrogates ought to have the authority to consent to nontherapeutic research under limited circumstances, and if researchers ought to enjoy immunity for acting upon such a consent, we should recommend a change in the law. [OD/S, 2]

Hence, this new proposed statute. One has to wonder how one can even calculate "direct medical benefits" to groups or "classes" or to society. But it is interesting that here the Working Group was clearly aware that research for a group or "class" is considered as non-therapeutic research,

---

[23] See THE BELMONT REPORT, *supra* note 10, at 2-3.

and that it would not be considered "health care." However, the important point is that from now on, in all drafts dealing with "expected benefit research," the terms "direct medical benefit" and "medical best interests" can refer only to a group or a "class" *or* to an individual human subject. The terms "direct medical benefit" and "medical best interests" can also refer only to "no direct benefit" non-therapeutic research for "society," or for the advancement of scientific knowledge, etc. The citizens of Maryland should understand that.

In sum, up to this point, the traditional distinctions used in biomedical research using human subjects have been blurred by redefining and equating the following: standard medical care, with therapeutic research; non-therapeutic research for a "class," with therapeutic research; beneficence for a particular individual patient, with beneficence for a "class"; "slight increase over minimal risk" research with "high risk" research; an advanced directive for standard medical care, with an advanced directive for research participation; consent for a particular detailed research protocol, with consent for "research-in-general"; a risk/benefit ratio that refers to benefits to a particular individual patient, with a risk/benefit ratio which refers to benefits to groups or a "class." To put it mildly, such purely equivocal definitions of so many of these key medical research terms alone could render any and all informed consents and "substituted judgments" invalid. Clearly, the citizens of Maryland will have to be quite sophisticated about the controversies swarming within bioethics and with these deconstructed definitions in order to understand exactly what they are getting into or voting for.

Invalid risk/benefit ratios

Since no "decisionally incapacitated" patient, "consent agent," or IRB can possibly know what the actual "risks" are (e.g., in "expected benefit" research which contains no risk categories or in non-therapeutic "no expected benefit" research which has blurred the categories of "slight increase over minimal risk" with "high risk"), and since no one can know what the actual "benefits" would be to possible future "classes" of patients, to "society," or to the advancement of scientific knowledge, etc., no one can possibly calculate a valid risk/benefit ratio.

Invalid "substituted judgments"

If it is impossible to calculate a valid risk/benefit ratio, no "decisionally incapacitated" patient could possibly give a valid informed consent to sign such an Advanced Directive for Research Participation, nor could any "consent agent" possibly give a valid "substituted judgment" that the patient would have wanted to participate were he/she competent.

Legal accountability

The May draft purports that the courts will be essentially removed from any involvement in the participation of the "decisionally incapacitated" in such research, including high risk/non-therapeutic research. In fact, in both drafts there is a legal "immunity" clause which purports to shield all researchers, physicians, consent agents, IRB members, etc., from all civil or criminal liability if a patient should incur any harms or injuries while participating in any such research. This would even be in violation of the present OPRR regulations.[24] In effect, purportedly there would be no recourse or due process accorded any patient injured or harmed during his/her participation in any research protocol, including high risk therapeutic and non-therapeutic research. It is doubtful that such absolutions could effectively deprive research subjects of their state and federal constitutional rights, or insulate researchers, consenters or IRB members from litigation for infringement of those rights. Even, it would seem, a state that was complicit in the deprivation of those rights would subject itself to serious liabilities.

Follow-up care/compensation for harms

There are no provisions for any follow-up medical care or any compensation for harms and injuries to patients incurred while partici-

---

[24] See OPRR REGULATIONS, *supra* note 3, at 9 (section 46.116). The OPRR regulations therein state: "No informed consent, whether oral or written, may include any exculpatory language through which the subject or the representative is made to waive or appear to waive any of the subject's legal rights, or releases or appears to release the investigator, the sponsor, the institution or its agents from liability for negligence."

pating in any of this research, including high risk/no direct benefit research. This would even seem to violate at least the spirit of the present federal OPRR regulations. Their obvious importance is pointed out, for example, in the Nuremburg Code: "In every one of the experiments the subjects experienced extreme pain or torture, and in most of them they suffered permanent injury, mutilation, or death, either as a direct result of the experiments *or because of lack of adequate follow-up care*" (emphasis mine).[25]

Distortion of the principle of "justice"

Guaranteeing total civil and criminal legal immunity for researchers, physicians, consenters, and IRB's, while legally precluding all patients from any due process when harmed or injured while participating in any research protocols, and legally precluding any follow-up medical care or compensation for harms and injuries sustained during participation in research, are clear and obvious distortions of the principle of "justice." Clearly the "balance" is rather heavy on the side of the benefits and interests of researchers, drug companies, research institutions, etc., over the benefits and interests of the people of the State of Maryland who will be the participants in this research.

---

[25] Nuremburg Code, in EXPERIMENTATION WITH HUMAN BEINGS: THE AUTHORITY OF THE INVESTIGATOR, SUBJECT, PROFESSIONS, AND STATE IN THE HUMAN EXPERIMENTATION PROCESS (Jay Katz, 1972), at 306. See also OPRR REGULATIONS, *supra* note 3, at 10 (section 46.116[6]). The OPRR regulations therein state: "(6) for research involving more than minimal risk, an explanation as to whether any compensation and an explanation as to whether any medical treatments are available if injury occurs and, if so, what they consist of, or where further information may be obtained." See also President's Commission for the Study of Ethical Problems in Medicine and Biomedical and Behavioral Research, COMPENSATING FOR RESEARCH INJURIES: A REPORT ON THE ETHICAL AND LEGAL IMPLICATIONS OF PROGRAMS TO REDRESS INJURIES CAUSED BY BIOMEDICAL AND BEHAVIORAL RESEARCH: REPORT, Vol. 1, Washington, D.C. (1982), at 25-39. See also Aller, Sharav, Becker, and Shamoo and Irving, *supra* note 14.

Exceptions and waivers

Unless one were familiar with the federal OPRR regulations, one would not be aware that the IRB can waive any part of this proposed statute in the interests of the advancement of scientific knowledge, to obtain information that can not be obtained in any other way, for national security, etc.[26]

Emergency room research

There is explicit language in both drafts which puts this proposed statute in "sync" with the controversial new changes in the FDA's regulations concerning the waiving of informed consent by "incompetent" patients (physically or psychologically incompetent) in emergency room research.[27] These new changes in the FDA regulations have been harshly rejected even by many of the leaders within bioethics. Yet, they have just been swiftly incorporated into the federal OPRR regulations and thereby into the Common Rule. This language in the proposed statute would seem to put "decisionally incapacitated" patients in double-jeopardy for being human subjects of research, especially in the event that they happened to find themselves in emergency rooms after car accidents, medication reactions, drug over-doses, seizures, etc.

Conclusion

Despite efforts to ground their "ethical" considerations on the bioethics principles, or their appeal to "consensus" (which could obviously change depending on the composition of the members), the Working

---

[26] See OPRR REGULATIONS, *supra* note 3, at 46.116 (c)(d) and 46.117 (c).

[27] See Department of Health and Human Services, Food and Drug Administration, 21 CFR Parts 50, 56, 312, 314, 601, 812, and 814, PROTECTION OF HUMAN SUBJECTS; INFORMED CONSENT AND WAIVER OF INFORMED CONSENT REQUIREMENTS IN CERTAIN EMERGENCY RESEARCH; FINAL RULES, Federal Register (Wednesday, October 2, 1996). For a few of the comments on this recent waiver of informed consent by FDA and DHHS, see Levine, Biros, Iserson, and Karlawish, *supra* note 21; Gina Kolata, *U.S. ban on medical experiments without patient consent is eased*, THE NEW YORK TIMES, Nov. 5, 1996, at A1.

Group seems totally unaware that the bioethics principles on which they explicitly ground this proposed statute are widely interpreted, are contentiously disputed, are no longer practically operative, and are in fact normative and therefore biased and hardly "neutral" for our "pluralistic, democratic" society (the best kept secret in bioethics). Indeed even utilitarianism or "consensus ethics" is normative. Therefore, how can the Working Group justify imposing its normative ethical "positions" and "consensus opinions" on the rest of the citizens of Maryland by means of the legalization of these very highly controversial and defunct ethical theories and opinions? Neither legalization nor consensus makes a position, policy, or statute neutral *or* ethical. Nor should any such ethical theory or opinion be so legalized.

Even the most universal medical research ethics codes express that it is not sufficient for the end or goal of a past, present, or future research protocol to be good or beneficial for the "greatest number" or for the advancement of scientific knowledge in order for it to be ethical. Prior sound animal studies, the legitimacy of the purposes for performing the research, the scientific qualifications of the researchers, the inalienable rights of each individual human research subject, the validity of the informed consent processes, the designs of the protocols, the means used to attain those "beneficent" goals, the circumstances and conditions under which the research protocols are conducted, the integrity of the research data, the legal responsibilities of the researcher and the institutions, and the following up with medical care and compensations for harm must also be part of any ethical evaluation. And there are some research protocols which are inherently wrong — in fact, illegal — regardless of any risk/benefit ratios, even though human subjects, like Martha, have given their "valid" informed consents.

Neither Martha nor any other human being — "decisionally incapacitated" or otherwise — has such an absolute "duty" to be so purely altruistic as to take part in experimentation in order to advance scientific knowledge, to provide the means for finding better medications or cures for diseases for others, to obtain scientific information which can only be obtained by means of the invasion of their minds or bodies, or to aid the national security. Nor should such a "duty" be legislated into any law, whether local, state or federal.

Because "decisionally incapacitated" human subjects like Martha are human persons, with the same inherent rights as all other human beings, and because no human beings should be used as unethical means to any goals, no matter how lofty, and because of the obvious vulnerability of "decisionally incapacitated" persons to exploitation and their compromised ability to give truly meaningful informed consent and our inability to know certainly their desires to participate in medical research, and because of the past and on-going abuses involving research with the mentally ill,[28] and because the present system of protections for the mentally ill in research are wholly insufficient and inadequate and thus realistically unable to protect them, the more reasonable way of "respecting persons" would be to acknowledge that, in order to respect them as non-autonomous persons, only minimal risk specified research for the direct benefit of a particular patient could be ethically consented to, and then only if the research holds out at least as much direct benefit as available standard medical therapies, and only as consented to by a legitimate legally authorized representative. In any other research, participation should be authorized by a court of law.

This does not mean that research in mental diseases or any other mental disorders must come to a grinding halt — only that the process of "scientific progress" must be ethical as well as the intended goal, even if it takes a little longer.[29] This is not an "anti-scientific research" position. But it is an "anti-unethical scientific research" position. There is a difference. If to be concerned about the kind of unethical scientific research in this proposed statute is simply dismissed, as Assistant Attorney General Schwartz puts it, as a matter of "fundamental differences of perspective," then we surely have a problem.

---

[28] See Shamoo & Keay, *Ethical concerns about relapse studies*, CAMBRIDGE QUARTERLY OF HEALTHCARE ETH., Summer 1996, at 373-386 (1996); Nancy Kass & Jeremy Sugerman, *Are research subjects adequately protected? A review and discussion of studies conducted by the Advisory Commissions on Human Radiation Experiments*, K.I.E. JOURNAL, Sept. 1996, at 271-282.

[29] See Jay Katz, *"Ethics in neurobiological research with human subjects — final reflections,"* in Shamoo (ed.), *supra* note 7, at 329-335; Timothy J. Keay, *Approximating ethical research consent*, in Shamoo (ed.), *supra*, at 149-153. See also Jay Katz, *supra* note 20; Adina M. Newman, *Drug trials, doctors, and developing countries: toward a legal definition of informed consent*, CAMBRIDGE QUARTERLY OF HEALTHCARE ETH., Summer 1996, at 387-399; Paul S. Appelbaum, *Consent and coercion: research with involuntarily treated persons with mental illness or substance abuse*, 4 ACCT. IN RES. 69, 69-79 (1995).

Chapter Eight

Therapy:

Friend or Foe to Spiritual Values and the Sacraments

Rev. W. Jerome Bracken, C.P.

Many years ago the *Linacre Quarterly* published Father John Harvey's article, "Spiritual and Psychological Values in Therapy."[1] In that article, he shows the close relationship of these values and then calls for clergymen and psychiatrists (or psychologists or counselors) to obtain their client's consent so that they can co-operate in working for their client's benefit.

To facilitate this cooperation, Harvey deftly touches on many of the areas where their concerns intersect: shared values, due and undue influence on the client's values, the positive impact of moral goals on therapy and the negative impact of neuroses on morality, the need for psychological insight for moral development and the need for personal responsibility and virtue for psychological health, and finally the need for self-transcendence for both psychological health and spiritual development. Having addressed these areas, Harvey writes that:

> Both the clergyman and the psychiatrist (or psychologist or counselor) should make their common client aware of all his human dimensions and potentialities as he seeks to be a whole man. The contribution of each

---

[1] *Linacre Quarterly* 39 (August 1972): 176-185.

professional is important to the patient's self-understanding. Despite the difficulties of communication between the professions, persistent cooperative efforts should continue for the sake of the patient. (p. 185)

Such cooperation, however, has not always happened, as Harvey observed in a later article on masturbation.[2] It seems that what he said in his 1972 article is still true today. This lack of cooperation is not due so much to psychiatrists and clergymen having so little time to communicate with one another. Rather, the reason is that professionals remain "... unconvinced of the practical importance of collaboration." Not having obtained the consent of their common client to work together for his or her total well being, they have "... categorized the work of the psychiatrist and the work of the moralist into neat compartments, as if they could be separated, when in truth they cannot."[3]

I would like to suggest that in addition to this reason there is also, on the part of some clergymen, a suspicion that psychology can undermine true spiritual values and the whole mystery of God's grace and mercy. These concerns show up in questions about the relationship of therapy to spiritual direction and the sacrament of reconciliation. Does therapy become a substitution for confession? Does it remove or at least undermine a sense of sin and guilt? Does a reliance on therapy show a lack of confidence in God's grace to bring about peace and a genuine conversion of life? Is the use of abreaction therapy an invitation to sin again, since it asks the person to re-experience what was happening when he did sin in order to gain insight about his difficulty? Does not such focusing on one's self take one's focus off God and His mercy?

These concerns are not minor. However, they are not insurmountable. In the practical order the common client of the therapist and clergyman could give consent to their working together to resolve any of these issues when they arise. The purpose of this paper is to facilitate that communication by addressing these concerns from a theoretical point of view.

---

[2] "The Pastoral Problem of Masturbation," *Linacre Quarterly* 60 (1993): 2.

[3] Harvey, "Spiritual and Psychological Values in Therapy," 181 and 178.

Is the Mystery of God's Grace Undermined by Therapy?

First, there is the issue of God's grace. Therapy does not exclude its reality. Moreover, therapy itself can be an instrument of God's grace. Theoretically we know that God can give his grace at any time, anywhere, and through any medium. That means that grace can be operative in a therapeutic session as well as in the sacrament. The sacrament has the advantage of being both an infallible and an efficacious sign of God's saving grace,[4] but both realities can be instruments of God's grace. This means that the therapist, while not the minister of the sacrament, can be an instrument through whom God gives his grace to the client. The clergyman, for his part, must respect that. In fact, he needs to be aware that God, as both the creating and the saving God, often works through different causes to accomplish multiple effects.[5] It would not be out of character for God to give the person grace both through the therapeutic session and the sacrament, so that they work together in His bringing about the Kingdom of God.

The therapist, on the other hand, also needs to make an acknowledgment. There are forces operating within a person that are not just subterranean. Concepts, a sense of fair play, and love itself impinge on a person's behavior and not just unconscious needs. Cognitive therapy, after all, postulates the importance of a person's conceptualizations for

---

[4] Rahner, Karl and Herbert Vorgrimler, "Sacrament," in *Theological Dictionary* (ed. Cornelius Ernst., O.P.; trans. Richard Strachan) (New York: Herder and Herder, 1965), s.v. "Sacrament." The authors liken the sacraments to a solemn pledge of salvation. "Since this dispensation (the eschatological situation of salvation in Christ) is final, definitive, and victorious, the pledge of salvation it contains is absolute and is not, in its God-willed solemn validity, made dependent on the moral state of the human minister of the pledge ... nor is it efficacious in virtue of the disposition or intention of its recipient . ...The sacraments contain and communicate (as instrumental causes) the grace which they signify."

[5] God can and has worked this way. In his theology of the passion, Thomas Aquinas points to the benefit of God saving mankind through multiple causes and not just through a simple act of his grace giving mercy. "By bringing about this salvation through the life and death of his son, God gives an example of how much He loves mankind, ... Secondly ... He set us an example ...." (*Summa Theologica* 3. 46. 3)

achieving psychological growth. Also, more than one psychologist has noticed the power for change that falling in love brings about. So the therapist need not deny the power for change that falling in love can bring about when the source of that falling in love is God himself. "Scientific research is drawing attention to a dynamism which, rooted in the depths of the psychic being, would push man toward the infinite." It is "an independent force" which is "an affective impulse carrying man immediately to the Divine... ."[6] Moreover, the therapist needs to respect the ways a person can contact this God who loves. Prayer, good works, worship and taking part in the sacraments are such ways.

Not surprisingly then, a Jewish psychiatrist asked a religious sister, when experiencing her resistance to growth, "Sister, have you been praying?" He was quite aware of the power for change that prayer can have.[7]

Though the therapist and the spiritual director have their own autonomy, the reality of God's grace is neither confined to one nor excluded from either.

Is Therapy a Substitute for Confession?

The second issue is the specific relation between therapy and the sacrament of reconciliation. In the past, clergy have remarked, "A good confession is as good as a therapy session." Some clergymen have argued that the reason why confessions are down is that people, having lost their faith, are substituting therapy for the sacrament. While there is some truth in these opinions, they can lead to some false conclusions. Therapy is not meant to be a second class form of confession, and confession cannot take the place of therapy.

While it is true that both therapy and the sacrament involve a truthful self-assessment which is expressed to another person, the nature of this

---

[6] "On Psychotherapy and Religion," an address to the Fifth International Congress on Psychotherapy and Clinical Psychology, April 13. 1953, sections 30-31, 34-35. N.C.W.C. translation, quoted by Fr. Harvey in "Spiritual and Psychological Views of Therapy" (note 1, above).

[7] Recounted by Dr. Maria Valdes, a clinical psychologist who works with priests, ministers, and rabbis so that the patient can integrate the psychological and spiritual dimensions of his or her life.

confession is different. When done to the therapist, the person is seeking psychological freedom. That is, he is asking the therapist to help him get free of the forces that seem to overwhelm him and control his behavior. The task of the therapist is to enable him to bring these forces into consciousness so that the client can deal with them. Honest self-assessment and self-revelation are the pathways by which this can happen.

When, however, the penitent confesses the sins of his life, he is doing something quite different. He is dealing with his own freedom. He is acknowledging he has misused it and is sorry. He is seeking forgiveness from God and guidance how not to commit sin again. The task of the confessor is not to bring him to freedom but to help him exercise his freedom well. His role is not to provide therapy, but to instruct him so he can form his conscience better and to offer absolution, so that God enters more deeply into his life. The clergyman also has the role of helping the penitent make and keep a firm purpose of amendment, so that his discipleship of Christ deepens.

The sense of relief that is experienced in these different sessions, while similar, can be distinguished. In the therapeutic session the person has been troubled by conflicts of which he is unaware but which cause him to act in dysfunctional ways. When this conflict comes into consciousness, he can experience relief. At last, what was not known, is now known; what he could not face, he can face now. He might even experience relief at the insight of seeing why he was acting that way. He has hope he can do something about it.

The penitent on the other hand experiences another kind of relief. His source of conflict is not at the unconscious level, but at the level of his conscience. Previous to confession he has kept his violation of conscience secret. In confession he releases this secret to another human being. What he did wrong, he is finally admitting. His conscience, which is always seeking truth, is now getting him to speak the truth, that is, confess his wrongdoing. The truthfulness and honesty which he had stonewalled by keeping his wrong doing secret is now being allowed to flow out of his very being. Such a release brings relief. It can also bring gratitude, since not only is his admittance of wrong accepted but his wrong doing is forgiven by God.

The therapist tries to bring his client to freedom; the clergyman tries to help the penitent use that freedom to follow Christ.

Does Therapy Remove a Sense of Sin and Guilt?

Another problem that seemingly can threaten a person's spiritual life is guilt. On the one hand, popular psychology paints guilt as an outright evil. Its stereotypical example is the guilt ridden, ritualistic, religious person, who is unable to enjoy life. So, pop psychology concludes that guilt has to be eliminated before a person can truly live. Sometimes, religion is perceived as a roadblock.

On the other hand, spiritual directors are often surprised if not perplexed when their directee does not seem to have a sense of sin or guilt. Should they be religious or seminarians, it seems as if the Church teaching they received reached no further than their final exam. When this occurs, it is tempting to conclude that psychology, not theology, has become their new anthropology.

Before the therapist and clergyman become adversaries over this, they would do well to examine the matter mutually. A sense of sin and guilt is not a simple phenomenon.

As a feeling, guilt can be described as a sense that one has missed the mark. One misses the mark either by going too far and overindulging[8] or by not going far enough in living up to what one should be doing. Where the complexity comes is in the feedback mechanism itself. The mechanism is either one's superego or one's conscience or both. Either or both can set the mark. The problem is that both these mechanisms can be well or ill formed.

Take one's conscience. When the mark is set by one's conscience, it is set by a careful consideration of the facts of the situation, the appropriate principles involved, and one's own ability to respond. Only then does one come to a judgment of what he or she should or should not do. In Grisez's words, conscience is one's last best judgment as to what should or should not be done.[9] When one violates this judgment, he or she experiences guilt. It is a moral guilt, since it comes from one's own

---

[8] Benedict M. Ashley, O. P. and Kevin D. O'Rourke, O. P., *Health Care Ethics: A Theological Analysis* (St. Louis, MO: The Catholic Health Association of the United States, 1982), 354.

[9] Germain Grisez, *The Way of the Lord Jesus* (Chicago: Franciscan Herald Press, 1983), Vol. 1 - *Christian Moral Principles*, 76.

judgment of conscience. In this case, guilt is the corrective response of conscience itself.[10]

The problem with conscience, however, is that it can be ill-formed. For instance, in his article about masturbation, Harvey writes that "many priests, seminarians and teachers of religion in our Catholic schools regard even the habit of masturbation as a non-issue, or perhaps as a purely psychological problem."[11] One could attribute this judgment to a certain kind of ignorance of Church teaching. While the *Catechism of the Catholic Church* acknowledges that certain psychological or social factors can "lessen if not even reduce to a minimum moral culpability,"[12] nonetheless, it also teaches that both "the Magisterium of the Church, in the course of a constant tradition, and the moral sense of the faithful have been in no doubt and have firmly maintained that masturbation is an intrinsically and gravely disordered action."[13]

As a result of this teaching being overlooked, no support is given to any natural sense that masturbation is morally wrong.[14] But then an absence of a sense of sin and of consequent guilt would be the fault of this person's religious teachers rather than the fault of therapy.

---

[10] Thomas Aquinas, *Summa Theologica*, 1-2. 87. 1. "Consequently, whatever rises up against an order, is put down by that order or by the principle thereof. And because sin is an inordinate act, it is evident that whoever sins, commits an offense against an order: wherefore he is put down in consequence, by that same order, which repression is punishment. Accordingly, man can be punished with a three fold punishment corresponding to the three orders to which the human will is subject .... Wherefore he incurs a three fold punishment; one inflicted by himself, viz., remorse of conscience ...."

[11] Harvey, "Masturbation," 34.

[12] *Catechism of the Catholic Church* (Liguori, MO: Liguori Publications, 1994), # 2352, as revised.

[13] *Catechism*, #2352, This is a quotation from the Congregation of the Doctrine of the Faith's document, *Persona humana* ("The Declaration on Certain Questions Concerning Sexual Ethics") #9.

[14] Harvey, "Masturbation," 35. As Harvey observes, "in spite of all the brainwashing from our culture many youngsters have the uneasy feeling that masturbation is wrong."

On the other hand, there can be a neurotic, rather than a real or moral, sense of guilt. In certain instances this kind of guilt hinders rather than helps a person's freedom to do good. It can arise when the superego alone sets the mark.

The superego is that part of the person's psyche, which, as the person was growing up, collected and internalized the judgments and commands of others. Their thinking and restraints substituted for the person's thinking and choosing that was still in the developing stage. The parent or teacher can tell the young person, "It's not right to miss Mass on Sunday." When these words are internalized, they become a rule of conduct, which, if broken under any circumstance, produces a sense of guilt.

Of course when the superego's directive is right for the occasion, and the person does not follow it, the consequent guilt is appropriate. But the guilt that arises from the superego is not always appropriate. When not made a part of one's own reasoning process, the superego's directive acts in an absolutist fashion, without regard to circumstances and the rule's applicability. So when a mother experiences guilt for missing Mass on Sunday while taking care of a sick daughter, her guilt is not founded in reality. It is neurotic. Moreover, if her fear of experiencing guilt becomes very strong, she could very well abandon her sick child and go to Mass. It is this kind of guilt that is detrimental for the person and for others. It should be eliminated.

Then whose job is this — the therapist or the spiritual director? It depends. If the source of the guilt is conscious, then it can be related to the person's conscience. The spiritual director can instruct this person so he can properly form his conscience. The guilt is coming from an erroneous conscience.

But the source of the guilt can be rooted in the unconscious as well. Try as a spiritual director or confessor might in instructing the person about what is sin or not sin, he will discover the person is intractable. As far as the person is concerned, he has but two options: either give up making judgments all together, or suffer the unrelenting tortures of guilt. Why? Because such judgments are not from any process of reasoning but from the person's unconscious, over which he has no control. In this case the skills of the therapist are needed so that the sources of conflict can be brought to the level of consciousness and worked through properly.

At this point the therapist and the spiritual director need to work hand in hand. They both can question the person about his behavior, asking him why he did it and encouraging him to explore why. They both can encourage him to act reasonably. Where their roles become distinct from one another is in how they help him to do this.

While encouraging his client to think and act consistently with his conscience, the therapist cannot propose his own value system as a basis for forming that conscience. That would be tantamount to making the client into the image and likeness of the therapist. When the therapist sees his client confused or thinks he is mistaken about his values, he not only can, but should, advise his client to seek counsel on this.

The role of the clergyman is to provide that counsel. What is important to know, however, is that the value system he proposes is not the spiritual director's own; it is that of the faith community. As mediator of that community, the spiritual director or clergyman addresses the problem at hand by presenting the moral wisdom of that community. In this way, instead of the person receiving a value system that is idiosyncratic to the therapist or even to the spiritual director, the person receives a value system that arises from his faith community, of which he or she is a member and through which the person can make his or her own judgments of right and wrong.

The role of the therapist in this regard is to make the person capable of living in community, making conscious what is not conscious, and encouraging him to be consistent in heart, in mind, and in action. The clergyman's role is to introduce the person into the specific community of which he or she is a member and instruct him or her about living in that community. In other words, the spiritual director's role is to help the person form a Christian conscience and live according to it.

Does Therapy Mean That Grace Is Not Sufficient?

One might ask, "Is therapy really necessary?" Could not God's grace enable the person to overcome his neurotic behavior?" Of course the answer is, "It could." But God often does not work this way, as anyone dealing with a scrupulous person has experienced. That person goes to confession countless times, seeking to get rid of his guilt, but never finds relief. In this case therapy is necessary, since one should not use the sacrament to solve a psychological problem.

A similar concern can be raised about the person's purpose of amendment. Is grace not sufficient for the person to carry out his purpose of amendment? It is. But here again the problem of sin is not wholly in the will. A person can firmly resolve, with the help of God's grace, to never sin again, yet find himself committing the same sin again and again. Why? Because God's grace in not sufficient? No, God's grace is always sufficient. Wherever there is freedom to be exercised, God's grace is offered. However, freedom rests on awareness and choice. And there can be sources of one's sinfulness of which one is not aware and, therefore, over which one has no control.

These hidden drives constitute part of the temptation of sin. But since the person is not aware of these aspects of temptation, he has no way of overcoming them. Using God's grace, he fights against what he knows. But he makes no defense against the other aspects of his temptation. For instance, while one young man knew he was drawn into a homosexual encounter because of his desire for sexual pleasure, he did not know that his need for power to withstand a woman's sexual abuse in his own home was also drawing him into that encounter. He was seeking not just sexual pleasure but sexual power. To amend, he sought to fight against the waves of sexual temptation but was unaware of the undertow of his need for power.

Of course, in any given moment — with God's actual grace and human co-operation — the person can withstand that temptation. But he will continue to walk into areas of temptation, without even knowing that he is doing so. Of course, the spiritual director might recognize the pattern of both where and when the temptation of a homosexual encounter occurs and warn the person of that. For instance, if the sexual encounters occur on the person's off day and when he goes to the mall, the spiritual director can warn him not to go there at that time. But this solution does not address the problems of when and how he is going to shop and socialize, nor does it address the other underlying reason why that time and place are so tempting to begin with. As those dealing with the somewhat similar problem of alcoholism know, a geographical solution is never sufficient. Until the "disease of the disease"[15] is addressed (save a miracle of grace), it is only a matter of time before a

---

[15] This phrase about the sickness of the sickness needing to be addressed comes from a conversation with Msgr. Dr. Andrew Cusack about alcoholism. He explained that first the alcoholic behavior has to be stopped, but then the sickness that generated the alcoholic behavior in the first place has to be cured.

fall occurs again.[16] In the case above, the disease of the disease is seeking to meet a need for power in the wrong way, that is, through a homosexual encounter.

Recognizing that God expects us to use human as well as divine means to live the spiritual life, the clergyman would encourage the person to enter therapy. In this way he would be able to discover what these unconscious causes of his sinning are. In the mean time, the clergyman would fulfill his role of instructing and encouraging the person to practice self-discipline, avoid the occasions of sin, pray, and do good works. In this, the therapist should rightly concur, since the easiest step in overcoming the person's dysfunction (even though very difficult for the client) is first to get him to stop the dysfunctional behavior. Addressing his confused thinking and bringing to consciousness the forces driving the behavior is more difficult and takes much longer.

Does the Abreactive Method of Therapy Lead to Sin?

Another cause for clergyman's concern are some of the methods of therapy itself. Could they unnecessarily jeopardize the person's spiritual life? Particularly problematic is the method of abreaction.[17] On the one hand the method is geared to bringing to the person's conscious level the causes of the behavior he wishes and should wish to stop, since it is

---

[16] In speaking about temptation, Lonergan says: "Deliberate vigilance can succeed for a time, but not for the whole time, nor ever for a long time. If only he puts his mind to it, the sinner can resist every temptation. But he cannot constantly be putting his mind to it." Bernard J. F. Lonergan, *Grace and Freedom: Operative Grace in the Thought of St. Thomas Aquinas* (ed. J. Patout Burns) (New York: Herder and Herder, 1971), 51.

[17] Ashley and O'Rourke, *Health Care Ethics*, 343-344.

gravely wrong.[18] On the other hand, the method has the appearance of tempting the person over again.

Again the spiritual director and therapist have to talk this out. Strictly speaking, the goal of abreaction is insight not action. That is, the therapist directs the person to re-experience the feelings and thoughts that accompanied the encounter. The reason for doing so is that out of experience comes insight.[19] The method is not meant to generate either a repeat of the behavior nor an interior choice for it. If such occurs then the therapeutic purpose is defeated. Instead of gaining insight into these disturbing feelings, the person gets rid of them quickly by acting them out — interiorly, if only by choice, or exteriorly, if also by action. Furthermore, by acting on his impulses he not only avoids facing these drives within himself but he also imbeds them more deeply in his mind and body.

---

[18] I use the term "gravely wrong" rather than the term "mortally sinful" advisedly. While every mortal sin must meet the condition that the act is gravely wrong, not every act that is gravely wrong is mortally sinful. The reason is that two further conditions must be met: sufficient reflection and full consent of the will. The homosexual encounter, according to Church teaching, is gravely wrong, removing the two positive values of the sexual act, loving union and procreation. However, there can be question whether this sexual encounter meets the condition of full consent. Full consent is not just a movement towards sexual pleasure, which is definitely taking place in this encounter, but is also an ability to determine to whom that movement should be directed and even whether it should be followed or not. The compulsion could be so great in this instance that the person no longer has this ability of self-determination or choice. Without this choice there is no full consent, no mortal sin.

[19] Thomas Aquinas says that insight arises from a conversion of the agent intellect on the phantasm. Bernard Lonergan says it is a grasp of the intelligibility in the experience. See his *Insight: A Study of Human Understanding* (New York: Philosophical Library, 1967), 500-501. He describes the process of full consciousness as a movement from experience, to understanding, to judgment and finally to decision. See his "Cognitional Structure" in *Collection: Papers by Bernard Lonergan, S.J.* (ed. F.E. Crowe, S.J.) (New York: Herder and Herder, 1967), 232-236. The method of the therapist, then, is to bring the person back to the point of experience so that instead of skipping understanding and judgment and going into action, he seeks to understand and judge before any action takes place.

What the spiritual director needs to know, then, is how this method is not going to lead the person back into sin but serve as a way out of temptation. His asking the therapist about this can lead them together to construct a strategy that insures both the therapeutic purpose and the person's spiritual growth.

The therapist can say that he would instruct the person about the method of abreaction — what its purpose is and how best that purpose can be achieved. For instance to help a person gain insight into his sexual desires and find what is setting them off in the wrong direction, the therapist suggests the person watch a movie that contains some love scenes. This would give him an opportunity to attend to all the different feelings he has when these sexual desires arise. These feelings arise from unmet needs. If the person opens himself to these feelings, he can discover what these needs are. Then he can work out ways to respond to these needs that are beneficial rather than dysfunctional. Moreover, he will discover that his needs are not simply sexual ones. By viewing this video in a therapy session, he has a way of insuring that instead of his acting out his drives he will learn to bring them more and more into his awareness, where he can better understand their nature and make good choices in their regard. In other words, the therapist sets forth the purpose and the process in such a way that, in moral terms, neither the end of abreactive therapy nor the means itself is wrong.

The spiritual director could make his suggestions as well. He judges the process in moral terms and concludes that watching such a film is an occasion of sin. He knows that one is morally obliged to avoid the near occasions of sin.[20] But he also knows that one can enter into an action, not evil in itself, for a good purpose if the good effects are proportionate to the evil effects. The evil effect for the person would be his arousal, to which he could fully consent and thereby sin. The good effect would be his overall experience, including his arousal, in so far as it offers him the possibility of a new insight and thus greater ability to confront his needs without sinning.

As stated above, abreaction therapy is an action that is not sinful in itself. What must be done is to make this occasion of sin a remote

---

[20] Denzinger and Schönmetzer, *Enchiridion Symbolorum: definitionum et declarationum de rebus fidei et morum*. Editio xxxll (Romae: Herder, 1963), 2161-2163.

occasion of sin. The spiritual director can instruct the person that this can be done by using both natural and supernatural means. He can encourage the person to adopt the procedures the therapist has proposed. They are good, natural ways of making the procedure a remote occasion of sin. He can further advise the person to do a number of spiritual things. He can suggest that he pray before such an action is done so he will keep to its good purpose, that he choose beforehand to deny himself whatever is in the pleasurable experience which would lead him into sin, and that he undergo the exercise not only in the presence of the therapist, who will help him to focus on gaining insight rather than on acting out, but also in the presence of Christ, who will help him consent[21] to what is good in the experience and not to what is evil.

Of course the spiritual director has to be quite clear about sexual pleasure itself. It is good when its experience leads one to affirm rather than deny the goods of marriage. That is, one's thoughts and choices must affirm that genital sexual pleasure is ordered to a mutual, exclusive, and life-time commitment of a man and woman together which is open to the generation of children. We can easily see how these are affirmed by a married couple when in being open to children they engage in sexual intercourse. But these goods can also be affirmed by refusing to procure genital pleasure when it is not open to children and when it does not involve an exclusive permanent relationship with a person of the opposite sex. The person has this second way of affirming the goods of marriage when watching the video. When the genital pleasure manifests itself, the person should acknowledge this pleasure and its desirability and then choose not to enter into it, but to move on to attending to the other feelings he is experiencing. As Eve could have chosen not to eat the fruit when she knew it was "good for food, ... a delight to the eyes, and ... to be desired to make one wise" (Gen 3:6), so can the person say "no" in the face of a similar attractiveness.

---

[21] One of the three conditions for committing mortal sin is described by the term "full consent." It might help to realize that full consent refers not to the spontaneous movement towards any perceived good, in this case, genital pleasure, but rather to the subsequent movement of choosing. What is full consent, in this case, would be the person choosing to stay with the genital pleasure he is experiencing rather than choosing to move to another level of what he is experiencing in watching such a video such as a need for affection or affirmation.

This therapeutic procedure, moreover, is directly helping the person to grow spiritually. First, by gaining insight into his needs, the person is acquiring self-knowledge, which is a foundation for a good spiritual life. Second, the person is helping himself spiritually in the very process he undergoes. When he goes through these experiences, he is making choices. By choosing not to stay with the genital pleasure he is experiencing and going to examine another feeling, the person is making a much stronger choice than simply saying no to sexual pleasure. His choice is a two-tiered one. First, he is saying no rather than yes to the genital pleasure. Second he is moving himself to another feeling rather than staying with the genital pleasure. Because this choice is much stronger than a simple act of self-denial, the continuous making of such choices while in the therapeutic session helps to form a habit. Since the habit is ordered to self-knowledge and self-regulation rather than to self-gratification, the habit is a good one. It is virtue. Thus, in addition to getting at sources of temptation which he was unable to get at before, the person, by this therapeutic process, is actually growing in virtue.

In fact the kind of virtue he is acquiring is that of chastity. Differing from continence, which simply excludes sexual pleasure, chastity acknowledges the sexual pleasure and directs it properly. Whereas continence generates a rational choice in the face of sexual pleasure, chastity acts as a full-body virtue, in which the multiple affects of the person and not just the will are embodied in the choice for what is good. By involving the body as well as the mind in the choice, chastity is a much stronger virtue than continence.

Thus, from this abreactive therapy, the person learns to address the multiple causes of his dysfunctional and sinful behavior. What he learns from this can be reenforced by the clergyman or spiritual director. Together with the therapist, the spiritual director can encourage the person to meet his other needs in a wholesome way. He can also show him that when his needs are not met at a particular time or in a particular way, he can turn this into an act of free self-denial.

Does Therapy Make One Concentrate on Self Rather Than God?

Even considering the benefit of gaining self-knowledge and developing the virtue of chastity, one can still ask if the person should, necessarily, undergo such therapy. Should not this focus on himself and his past sinfulness be changed to a focus on God's mercy? One could argue that, by dwelling on his guilt, the person unduly disturbs himself and loses peace as well as hope.

In response to these objections, we need to consider that the underlying concern is one of conversion, a turning from sin to God. Therapy, of course, is not necessary for this. God's grace alone can bring the person to turn from sin to Him. However, conversion is a human, as well as a divine, phenomenon. Besides grace urging us to relate to God, the very nature that God created in us urges us to do this.[22] By his own plan, then, God wanted our conscience to disturb us when we do not do what is right. He wanted it to disturb us not only when we do not hit the mark, but also when we do not do our part to hit the mark. So it is His plan that we look to our own purpose of amendment, as well as to His grace, to stop falling into sin. If the strategy for our purpose of amendment is not working, then we are obliged, by our own nature and by grace, to find a strategy that works. The self-reflective process of therapy can become the strategy we must use in order to stop doing wrong.

When would this occur? When one's own attempts to change one's behavior and acquire a rightly formed conscience fail to stop the objectively sinful actions. Why? Because human acts involve not only our behavior, not only our thoughts and choices, but also our emotions, both conscious and unconscious. Should the person be able to stop his sinful behavior, he fulfills his obligation of not doing wrong, though he stills needs to do what is right to complete his spiritual conversion. However, if the person fails to stop his sinful behavior, then he must address the problem at its next level of causality, that of thinking and choosing. Should this procedure fail, then in order to be responsible and not do what is objectively wrong, the person is obliged to get at the unconscious causes of his behavior.[23] Prayer for God's grace might be all that is required for this to happen. But if calling upon the supernatural does not work, then one must call upon natural means to get at the unconscious causes of one's sinful behavior. In this case therapy could be considered an ordinary means by which to cooperate with God's grace.

---

[22] In Romans (2:15-16) Paul describes every person as searching for God and needing to obey God speaking within his or her heart. *Gaudium et spes* (#16) speaks of a person's conscience residing in his or her heart to do right.

[23] This is Dr. Maria Valdes' idea and practice in her therapeutic approach.

Why? Because one moves to God not only by grace but also by one's free actions. The more one expands one's freedom, the more natural resources one has to move to God. Freedom is expanded at the cognitive and at the affective levels of our being. The more aware we become, the more options we see; the greater the power we utilize, the greater our freedom to choose these options. Therapy enables a person to bring into consciousness ideas, instincts, and emotions that have been repressed. Consequently, the person attains a greater awareness of himself. Also, by bringing into consciousness the ideas and forces that have influenced his behavior, but in a dysfunctional way, the person can correct the errors in these ideas and redirect these instincts and emotions to their proper goals. Thomas Aquinas makes the astute remark that just as moral goodness is expanded when one's inner choice moves to an external action, so, too, is moral goodness expanded when one is moved to what is good not only by one's will but also by one's emotions.[24] Therapy which helps us to get at our repressed emotions and instincts, therefore, becomes a way by which we can attain a greater freedom and power to act morally and thus, with God's grace, come closer to Him.

Conclusion

By carefully addressing the charges that therapy can harm the spiritual and sacramental life of the person, we can draw the following conclusions. While God's grace works through the sacraments it can extend beyond the sacraments and make therapy an instrument of grace. While there is the similar practice of confession and the similar experience of relief in therapy and the sacrament of reconciliation, they occur in different areas of one's psyche and for different reasons. The first is to enable the person to come into freedom; the second is to enable the person to use his or her freedom for Christ.

With regard to a sense of guilt and a sense of sin, therapist and clergyman must recognize the complexity of these phenomena, their different roles in dealing with them, and also their shared though distinct responsibilities. Each in his or her own way is to lead the person away from an inappropriate to an appropriate sense of sin and guilt, lest the person never reach his full psychological and spiritual well being. While the grace of God is always sufficient to lead the person from sin to the

---

[24] Aquinas, *Summa Theologica*, 1-2. 24. 3.

practice of virtue, God himself does not disdain human freedom and the ordinary means of enhancing that freedom so that this can come about.

Thus, while affirming the power of God's grace, the clergyman must encourage his client to use ordinary means to cooperate with God's grace, including therapy. The therapist for his part, needs to recognize the recent research about spiritual activities contributing to a person's psychological health and therefore not disdain these means as unable to contribute to his therapeutic goal. In addition the therapist needs to recognize how the spiritual and moral assistance that the clergyman offers to his patient can actually facilitate both the use and success of abreactive therapy. At the same time, the clergyman needs to see how this method can actually help his client grow in the practice of virtue, such as the virtues of continence and chastity. Finally, the clergyman needs to recognize that therapy's concentration on self-awareness and self-reflection need not be a way of turning one's attention away from God but a way of expanding those natural components of awareness and choice by which one co-operates with the grace of God in following Christ.

After all, in the sacrament of reconciliation, the penitent needs to reflect on himself so as to be able to confess to wrong-doing, to be sorry for it, and to take those steps necessary for a firm purpose of amendment. Rather than being inimical to these practices, therapy can assist them. Rather than being purely human practices, the sacrament of reconciliation can make this self-reflection, sorrow, and redirection integral to the person's repentance for sin and discipleship of Christ. The Word of God need not stop at Christ's incarnation but can become incarnate in all our endeavors.

Postscript

Thoughts from a Former Student

Dr. ROSALIND EDMAN SMITH
(Dunbarton College of the Holy Cross, Class of '64)

Never could I have imagined, forty years ago, that I would be writing a "postscript" to a book celebrating the life and work of John Francis Harvey, OSFS. It is an honor and a privilege. Let me first establish my "credentials" for this august assignment.

As a student at Dunbarton College of Holy Cross (Washington, D.C.), I was one of hundreds of "Dunbarton girls" who were taught moral theology by Father Harvey. With his acute mind, (and his glasses moving from one part of the desk to another), he challenged us to use our reason in reflecting upon faith – no small awakening for many of us in the early sixties. Little did I know then that our paths would continue to cross for the next four decades. But, then, little did I know Father Harvey!

Student days ended and several years passed. I returned to Dunbarton as a lecturer in the theology department, chaired by Father Harvey. Those were the years when theology and philosophy departments were struggling to maintain their primacy in the curriculum. And struggle Father did. Those were also the years during which the Congregation of the Holy Cross was determining whether Dunbarton College should continue to be part of their college apostolate. They were painful years for all involved, and not least for Father Harvey. Father never fails to remind me that it was I who broke the news to him, that the decision had been made to close the College and concentrate the community's resources in its larger college, St. Mary's (Notre Dame, IN).

When Dunbarton closed, Father Harvey had been teaching there for twenty-five years. He could recall just about every graduate by name (and still can!). His love and devotion to the College and to the Dunbarton alumnae continue to this day. I can still see Father at the final graduation, sitting on the outdoor stage, flanked by his friend Reverend Walter Burghardt, S.J., the commencement speaker. It was a painful moment.

More years passed. Those of us who had been at Dunbarton when it closed in 1973 found ourselves scattered in many different directions. Father continued to teach at De Sales School of Theology, to write, and to become increasingly more immersed in his new apostolate to persons striving to live in accord with the Church's pastoral teachings on homosexuality.

In 1990, I became a member of the Department of Philosophy & Theology at Allentown College of St. Francis de Sales (now DeSales University) in Center Valley, Pennsylvania. To my surprise and delight, I discovered that Father Harvey was now teaching in Center Valley! In addition to his many speaking, writing, and counseling responsibilities, he had continued his college teaching ministry begun at Dunbarton in 1948.

And Father had not changed one iota. As those of you who know him can attest, his appearance, his "wild (well, twinkling!) Irish eyes" and ready smile have changed barely, if at all, in the past four decades. Even more amazing, his energy level, now, three years after the Golden Jubilee of his Ordination, seems only to increase! Today, he continues to teach, preach, write, counsel, travel, and in all ways minister to the People of God. We sometimes jokingly refer to him as the "Energizer Bunny."

But, to the more important "postscript"... John Francis Harvey is a scholar, an author, a teacher, a spiritual director, and a friend. But, foremost, he is an Oblate of St. Francis de Sales. His life roles as scholar, author, teacher, spiritual director and friend are simply the prisms that reflect the brightness of the image of St. Francis de Sales, the model and founder of the Oblate Community. Turning to the *Constitutions* of the Oblates of St Francis de Sales, referred to as the "law of love" for the members of that religious congregation, we gain a more profound understanding of Father Harvey.

There, the members of the Oblate community are reminded that *zeal* was St. Francis de Sales' most outstanding virtue.

His ministry was characterized by a joyful optimism, confident in the effectiveness of God's grace and believing in the good which is in the human person. For him there was no barrenness on earth that the charity of the priest could not render fruitful in some way.

It is Father Harvey's zeal, joyful optimism, confidence in the effectiveness of God's grace, and belief in the good which is in the human person that have fueled his priestly ministry for more than fifty years. How else might we understand someone whose "zeal for souls" continues to take him from city to city, country to country, even, recently, to Australia, after three-score and twenty years?

Reflecting on the *Constitutions* in an address to the Major Superiors of the Oblates, the Superior General, Reverend Lewis Fiorelli spoke of the "Oblate Ministry of Compassion."

*Oblate ministers are to enjoy being **with** the people they serve, taking the initiative to be among them so as to serve them. Like the Good Shepherd,* he said, they are *to know* [their] *sheep by name.*

(Father Harvey has taken this last directive quite literally, remembering by name students he taught in the 1950's!)

They are to serve [their] *people with a gentleness which is unfeigned and which finds its strength in the gentle heart of Christ. They are to go out in search of them.*

How very descriptive this is of Father Harvey. I cannot help but think of the many times over the years that Father Harvey has traveled by plane, train, or automobile to New York, Washington, or wherever there has been a Dunbarton student in need. Certainly not *only* Dunbarton students have been the recipients of his ministry of compassion, but of these I know first-hand.

In speaking of the Oblate Life, the *Constitutions* note that

the Holy See 'asked us not to limit our works; ...not to isolate ourselves from the world; ... but, on the contrary, to be in continual contact with the world, to be involved with it' in order to bring it to Christ. 'The Oblates are thus called to enter society such as it is' and to make it Christian, "and this by every means possible."

In 1978 the late Terence Cardinal Cooke asked Father Harvey to come to the Archdiocese of New York to establish a spiritual support system for men and women with homosexual inclinations who wished to live in accord with the teachings of the Church. In 1980 *Courage* was born. This "ministry of compassion" is now a worldwide ministry, present in seven countries, twenty-eight states, and the District of Columbia and growing still. Father continues to travel to New York weekly to conduct one of the chapters of *Courage.*

Finally, perhaps the most profound understanding of Father Harvey can be found in the maxim of St. Francis de Sales: LIVE JESUS! St. Francis told his followers that if the gentle Jesus lived in their hearts, he would also live in their conduct and appear in their eyes, in their mouth, and in their hands (paraphrased). They would LIVE JESUS!

Father John Harvey, O.S.F.S., in his life, in his work, in his relationships LIVES JESUS!

Bibliography

The Legacy of a Moral Theologian: Rev. John F. Harvey, O.S.F.S.

(1) Professional Experience

Teaching

2000	Visiting Professor - Seton Hall University (NJ)
1997	Visiting Professor - Seton Hall University (NJ)
1987-97	Adjunct Professor - Allentown College of St. Francis de Sales (PA)
1979	Visiting Professor - Theological Union (Australia and New Zealand)
1976	Visiting Professor - Diocesan Seminary in Melbourne (Australia)
1948-87	Professor - De Sales School of Theology (DC)
1948-73	Associate Professor - Dunbarton College of the Holy Cross (DC)

Administration

1980 - present	Executive Director of *Courage*
1978-94	President of *Compulsion, Courage & Chastity*

Professional Memberships

American Society of Christian Ethics (1968-1980)

Catholic Theological Society of America (1950 - present)

College Theology Society (1953-1963)

Fellowship of Catholic Scholars (1978 - present)

Mariological Society of America (1955-1986)

Society of Catholic Social Scientists (1997 - present)

(2) Publications

Books

editor, with Gerald Bradley, of *New Perspectives Concerning Homosexuality, with Special References to the Rearing of Children* (tentative title), to be published by Our Sunday Visitor Press (2000)

The Truth about Homosexuality: The Cry of the Faithful (San Francisco: Ignatius Press, 1996). Also available in Polish, *Prawda o Homoseksualizmie* (trans. by Woxanie Wiernych, 1999)

editor of *Homosexuality: Challenges for Change and Reorientation* (Journal of Pastoral Counseling, 28; New Rochelle, NY: Iona College, 1993)

The Homosexual Person: New Thinking in Pastoral Care (San Francisco: Ignatius Press, 1987)

The Moral Theology of The Confessions of St. Augustine (Washington, DC: Catholic University of America Press, 1951)

Pamphlets

Courage: A Handbook (1991; revised 1995)

A Spiritual Plan to Redirect One's Life (Daughters of St. Paul, 1979)

Pastoral Care and the Homosexual (Knights of Columbus, n.d.)

Articles

2000

"Why the Church Opposes Domestic Partnerships" — forthcoming in *The Arlington Catholic* (January 2000).

1999

"Commentary," with Fr. Kazimierz Kowalski — *Catholic Eye* 163 (July 30, 1999), pp. 2-3; published by the National Committee of Catholic Laymen.

"Observations on the Vatican Decision Regarding Father Robert Nugent, SDS, and Sister Jeannine Gramick, SSND" — *Courage: The Newsletter*, vol. 99/4 (1999).

1998

"Observations on the Revised Version of 'Always Our Children'" — *Courage: The Newsletter*, vol. 98/3 (1998).

1997

"Observations on the Bishops' Committee's Letter 'Always Our Children'" — *Courage: The Newsletter*, vol. 97/4 (1997).

"Speaking Out with Courage" — *Crisis* (December 1997).

"The Pastoral Challenge of Homosexuality on a Catholic Campus" — *The Turnaround* (Cardinal Newman Society, 1997).

"Courage and Church Teaching" — *Catholic World Report* (July 1997), pp. 53-54.

"Developing into Heterosexuality" — *Ethics & Medics* 22/7 (July 1997).

"Pastoral Implications of Church Teaching on Homosexuality" — *Lay Witness* (March 1997).

1996

"Homosexual Orientation and Genetics" — *Ethics and Medics* (May 1996).

"An Interview with Fr. Harvey of Courage" — *Human Life International Report* (November 1996).

1993

"New Theories of Physical Causes of Homosexuality and Moral Behavior" (with Fred S. Berlin) — *Communicating the Catholic Vision of Life*, Proceedings of the Twelfth Bishops' Workshop in Dallas, Texas (1993).

"The Pastoral Problem of Masturbation" — *Linacre Quarterly*, 60/2 (May 1993).

"Sexual Abstinence for the Homosexual Person" — *Journal of Pastoral Counseling*, 28 (1993): 40-43.

"Updating Issues Concerning Homosexuality" — *Journal of Pastoral Counseling*, 28 (1993): 8-39.

1992

"Priests Who Stray" — *Crisis* (November 1992); reprinted in *Journal of Pastoral Counseling*, 28 (1993): 44-52.

1990

"Psychological and Pastoral Aspects of Sexual Addiction" — Proceedings of the Pope John XXIII Center (1990).

"Aspects of Addiction" — Proceedings of the Ninth Bishops' Workshop in Dallas, Texas (1990).

1989

"Reflections on Teaching Moral Theology: 1949-1989" — in *Salesian Reflections* (ed. William Ruhl; Washington, DC: De Sales School of Theology, 1989), pp. 75-77.

1988

"Homosexuality and Hope: New Thinking in Pastoral Care" — in *Hope for Homosexuality* (ed. Patrick Fagan; Washington, DC: Free Congress Foundation, 1988), pp. 65-77.

1980

"Expressing Marital Love During the Fertile Phase" — *International Review of Natural Family Planning*, 4/4 (Winter 1980)

"Homosexuality" *New Catholic Encyclopedia*, Vol. 17, Supplement, pp. 271-73. Original article in *New Catholic Encyclopedia*, 7:116.

"The Impact of Gay Propaganda Upon Adolescent Boys and Girls" — *The Priest* (March 1980)

1979

"The Morality of Masturbation" — *The International Journal of Natural Family Planning* (July 1979)

"Recent Trends in American Catholic Moral Theology"— *The Australian Catholic Record* (October 1979): 363-376

"Reflections on a Retreat for Clerics with Homosexual Tendencies" — *The Linacre Quarterly* (May 1979): 136-140.

1978

"Human Sexuality and the Homosexual: A Critique" — *Faith and Reason: The Journal of Christendom College*, 3 (1978)

1977

"Chastity and the Homosexual" — *The Priest* (July-August 1977).

"On Understanding Human Sexuality: A Critique of the CTSA Study" (with William E. May) — *Communio* (Fall 1977): 195-225. [Reprinted by Franciscan Herald Press]

"The Plan of Life for the Homosexual" — three articles in the *National Catholic Register* (September-October 1977)

"The Treatment of Homosexuality in the C.T.S.A. Report on Homosexuals" — *Communio* (Winter 1977): 389-391.

1976

"Contemporary Theological Views" — *Linacre Quarterly*, 43/3 (August 1976); reprinted in *Counseling the Homosexual* (ed. John R. Cavanaugh; Our Sunday Visitor Press).

"A Critique of John McNeill, S.J. and Gregory Baum, O.S.A. on the Subject of Homosexuality" — *Linacre Quarterly*, 43/3 (August 1976)

"Pastoral Insights on 'Sexual Ethics'" — *Pastoral Life*, 25/4 (April 1976)

1975

"Euthanasia: Commentary on a Social Movement" — *Linacre Quarterly*, 41/3 (August 1975)

"Law and Personalism" — *Communio*, 2/1 (Spring 1975)

1974

"Changes in Nomenclature and Their Probable Effect" — *Linacre Quarterly*, 41/3 (August 1974); reprinted in *Counseling the Homosexual* (ed. John R. Cavanaugh; Our Sunday Visitor Press).

"The Controversy Concerning Nomenclature Vis-a-Vis Homosexuality" — *Linacre Quarterly*, 41/3 (August 1974)

"Homosexual 'Marriages'" — *Marriage and Family Living* (January 1974)

1973

"The Controversy Concerning the Psychology and Morality of Homosexuality — *American Ecclesiastical Review*, 167/9 (November 1973)

1972

"Attitudes of a Catholic Priest Towards Homosexuality" — *Bulletin of the National Guild of Catholic Psychiatrists*, 18/1 (December 1972): 53-58.

"Integration of Spiritual and Psychological Values in Therapy" — *Linacre Quarterly*, 39 (August 1972)

1971

"Attitude of Priests Toward Homosexuals" — *The Bulletin of the National Guild of Catholic Psychiatrists* (May 1971)

"Homosexuality and Vocations" — *The American Ecclesiastical Review*, 164 (January 1971)

"Pastoral Directives for the Confessor in regard to Homosexuality" — *Linacre Quarterly* (August 1971)

"Pastoral Responses to Gay World Questions" — *Ethics, Theology and Homosexuality*, ed. W. Dwight Oberholtzer. (1971)

1970

"The Morality of Heart Transplants" — *The American Ecclesiastical Review*, 162 (April 1970)

1969

"Female Homosexuality" — *The Linacre Quarterly*, 36/2 (May 1969)

"The Meaning of *Humanae Vitae* and its Binding Force" — *The Bulletin of the National Guild of Catholic Psychiatrists*, 16/1 (January 1969)

"Moral Obligations in Catchetical Programs" — *The American Ecclesiastical Review*, 160/ 4 (April 1969)

1968

"The Morality Conference in St. Louis Revisited: A Critique of Charles Curran" — *Homiletic and Pastoral Review*, 69/1 (October 1968).

"Problems in Counseling the Married Homosexual" — *The American Ecclesiastical Review*, 158/2 (February 1968)

1967

"Homosexuality" — *New Catholic Encyclopedia* (1967)

"Morality and Pastoral Treatment of Homosexuality" — *Continuum*, 5 (Summer 1967)

"The Pastoral Treatment of Compulsion in the Homosexual" — *All Things to All Men*, vol. 2 (1967)

"The Pastoral Question of Homosexuality" — *All Things to All Men*, vol. 1 (1967)

"Selective Conscientious Objection" — *The American Ecclesiastical Review*, 159 (1967)

1964

"Alienation of the Homosexual from the Religious Community" — *ECHO* (October 1964)

1963

"Counseling the Apparent Adolescent Homosexual" — *Bulletin of the National Guild of Catholic Psychiatrists*, 10/4 (October 1963): 204-213.

1962

"Counseling the Religious Invert" — *Bulletin of the National Guild of Catholic Psychiatrists* (October 1962)

1957

"Techniques in Counseling: A Comparison of the Method of St. Francis de Sales with that of Carl Rogers' Client Centered Therapy" — *Catholic Educator* (part I, February 1957; part II, April 1957)

1955

"Homosexuality as a Pastoral Problem — *Theological Studies* (March 1955)

1950

"The Nature of the Infused Moral Virtues" — Vol. 10, *Proceedings of the Catholic Theological Society of America* (1950)

1949

"Self Criticism of the Priest-Professor" — *Catholic Educator* (December 1949)

Book Reviews

article on Germain Grisez, et. al., *The Way of the Lord Jesus, vol. 2: Living a Christian Life*, in *Homiletic and Pastoral review* 95/7 (April 1995): 72-77.

article on Elizabeth Moberly, *Homosexuality: A New Christian Ethic*, in *Linacre Quarterly* (November 1984)

article on Elizabeth Moberly, *Early Development of Gender Identity*, in *Linacre Quarterly* (May 1984)

article on Germain Grisez, *Christian Moral Principles, volume 1*, in *Homiletic and Pastoral Review* (August-September, 1984).

"Response to Malcolm Potts on Breastfeeding" in *International Review of Natural Family Planning*, 8/2 (Summer, 1984): 174-180.

"A Theological Reflection on Sex and Gender" in *Sex and Gender*, The Pope John Center, 1984, St. Louis, MO, pp. 340-349.

article on John Boswell's, *Christianity, Social Tolerance, and Homosexuality: Gay People in Western Europe from the Beginning of the Christian Era to the Fourteenth Century*, in *Linacre Quarterly* (1981).

review of *The Homosexual Question*, by Marc Oraison, in *Theological Studies* (1977)

review of *The Church and the Homosexual*, by John McNeill, SJ, in *Long Island Catholic* (10/7/76) and in *Theological Studies* (1977)

review of Robert T. Francoeur's, *Eve's New Rib*, in *American Ecclesiastical Review*, 167 (March 1973).

The Anthropology of Sex, by Abel Jeanniere, in *Theological Review* (June 1968): 184.

review of *Toward A Christian Understanding of the Homosexual*, by H. Kimball Jones, in *Theological Review* (September 1967): 160.

review of *Counseling the Invert*, by John R. Cavanagh, in *Theological Studies* (December, 1966)

review of *Sin, Liberty, and Law*, by Louis Monden, S.J.

review of *Marriage: A Psychological and Moral Approach*, edited by William C. Bier, S.J., in *Theological Studies* (December, 1965).

review of *Pastoral and Sexual Problems in Pastoral Theology*, edited by William C. Bier, S.J., in *Theological Studies* (March, 1965).

(3) Presentations

Lectures and Conferences

1999

"Pastoral Care of the Person with Same-Sex Attraction" — at The Wanderer Forum (*Homosexuality and the Catholic Church in Today's Culture*) in South Bend (IN), April 17, 1999.

"A Positive, Moral Approach to Homosexual Problems" — at the 8th Annual Northeast Regional Wanderer Forum (*Threats to Our Catholic Faith: The RENEW 2000 and Homosexual Initiatives*) in Albany (NY), March 27, 1999.

1997

"Homosexuality and Courage" — *Homosexuality and American Public Life* (Georgetown Conference Center), June 19-21, 1997.

1996

"Courage and Church Teaching" — *Call to Holiness* (Detroit, MI), November 16, 1996.

1993

"On the Church's Response to People Who Want to Overcome the Condition of Homosexuality" — Newman Club of the University of Virginia, April 1, 1993.

"On the Church's Response to People Who Want to Overcome the Condition of Homosexuality" — Jacques Maritain Club at Princeton University, March 15, 1993.

"Morality of Homosexual Activity and Prevalent Myths" — Mount St. Mary's Seminary, March 15, 1993.

"Prevalent Media Myths Concerning Homosexuality" — Seton Hall University, March 10, 1993.

"Moral Perspectives on the Origins of Homosexuality" (with Dr. Fred Berlin) — panel discussion for the Pope John XXIII Center

1990

"The Moral Aspects of Addiction from a Pastoral Perspective" — ninth Bishops' Workship in Dallas, Texas

1989

"Adolescents and Sexuality" — Devon Prep School in Devon, Pennsylvania

1988

presentation of Roman Catholic teaching on homosexuality at Opus Dei "think-tank" at Princeton University

Speaking Engagements on behalf of "Courage"

2000

keynote address for annual national conferenc

address at the University of Notre Dame, Indiana

address at St. Charles Borromeo Seminary, Pennsylvania

address at Christendom College, Virginia

address at Mount Saint Mary's Seminary, Maryland

address at the Michigan Family Forum

address to the "Parents and Friends Ministries" conference (Washington, DC)

address to the Knights of Columbus (Easton, MD)

1999

addresses sponsored by Human Life International, given in Australia

workshop in Tucson, Arizona

address in La Crosse, Wisconsin

workshop for priests in diocese of Jacksonville, FL
address to the Catholic Medical Association (Buffalo, NY)
address to the Catholic Medical Association (Chicago, IL)
address to the Notre Dame Law School (South Bend, IN)

1998

address for youth leaders at annual national conference
workshop at annual national conference
keynote address at annual national conference
address to priests in diocese of Jacksonville, FL
addresses sponsored by Human Life International, in New Zealand/Australia
address in Chicago, Illinois, sponsored by the Knights of Columbus
address at the Wanderer Forum in Milwaukee, Wisconsin
addresses at the Human Life International Conference in Clare, Ireland

1997

keynote address and workshop at annual national conference
workshop for diocese of Lincoln, NE
lecture in diocese of Charlotte, NC
lecture in diocese of Orlando, FL
address at chancery office, diocese of Norwich, CT
lecture at St. Charles Borromeo Seminary, Philadelphia, PA
lecture to Newman Club Chaplains, archdiocese of New York
lecture in parish of St. George, diocese of Trenton, NJ
lecture at Mount St. Vernon College, Riverdale, NY

1996

keynote address at annual national conference

1995

lecture at annual national conference

1993

address to Catholic laity in South London, England
address to priests in diocese of Leeds, England
address to priests and psychologists of the archdiocese of New York

Radio & Television Appearances

2000

television interview for "Focus" (New Orleans, LA)
radio program for "Peter's Voice" (Providence, RI)

1999

radio programs for "Peter's Voice" (Worcester, MA)
guest on "Living His Life Abundantly" (Eternal Word Television Network)
CBS News Sunday Morning

1998

radio program for "Catholic Answers" in California
public radio in Providence, RI
Catholic radio programs in Providence, RI
guest on "Mother Angelica Live" (Eternal Word Television Network)

1997

FOCUS (Franciscan University of Steubenville)
guest on "Living His Life Abundantly" (Eternal Word Television Network)
guest on "Mother Angelica Live" (Eternal Word Television Network)

(4) Honors & Awards

1988 *Cardinal Wright Award* (Fellowship of Catholic Scholars) - for outstanding service in the Church

1988 honorary *Doctor of Humane Letters* (Allentown College of St. Francis de Sales) - for pastoral work

1986 honorary *Doctor of Humane Letters* (Assumption College) - for pastoral writings on St. Augustine

1984 *Linacre Quarterly* Award - for distinguished writing